THE SEARCH FOR GOD, PURPOSE,
AND A MEANINGFUL LIFE

Young & BEARDLESS

THE SEARCH FOR GOD, PURPOSE, AND A MEANINGFUL LIFE

JOHN LUKE ROBERTSON

WITH TRAVIS THRASHER

THOMAS NELSON
Since 1798

Young and Beardless

Published in Nashville, Tennessee, by Tommy Nelson. Tommy Nelson is an imprint of Thomas Nelson. Thomas Nelson is a registered trademark of HarperCollins Christian Publishing, Inc.

The Duck Commander logo is used with permission.

Published in association with WME Entertainment, c/o Mel Berger and Margaret Riley King, 1325 Avenue of the Americas, New York, New York 10019.

Thomas Nelson titles may be purchased in bulk for educational, business, fund-raising, or sales promotional use. For information, please e-mail SpecialMarkets@ThomasNelson.com.

ISBN: 978-0-7180-8790-6

Library of Congress Cataloging-in-Publication Data:

Names: Robertson, John Luke, author.
Title: Young and beardless : the search for God, purpose, and a meaningful life / John Luke Robertson, with Travis Thrasher.
Description: Nashville : Thomas Nelson, 2016. | Includes bibliographical references.
Identifiers: LCCN 2016005469 | ISBN 9780718087906 (pbk.)
Subjects: LCSH: Robertson, John Luke. | Christian biography--Louisiana. | Television personalities--Louisiana--Biography. | Duck dynasty (Television program)
Classification: LCC BR1725.R618 A3 2016 | DDC 277.3/083092--dc23 LC record available at http://lccn.loc.gov/2016005469

Printed in the United States of America

16 17 18 19 20 RRD 6 5 4 3 2 1

To my family, who stands by me through all my craziness and encourages me to reach for the stars. Each one of you has played a role in teaching me to love the Lord with all my heart and in inspiring me to live my dreams. Thank you.

CONTENTS

FAMILY CAST OF CHARACTERS

DAD: Willie Robertson

MOM: Korie Robertson

PAPAW PHIL: Phil Robertson (grandpa, Dad's side)

MAMAW KAY: Kay Robertson (grandma, Dad's side)

2-PAPA: John Howard (grandpa, Mom's side)

2-MAMA: Chrys Howard (grandma, Mom's side)

MAMAW JO: Jo Shackelford (great-grandma, Mom's side)

PAPAW SHACK: Luther Shackelford (great-grandpa, Mom's side)

PAPAW HOWARD: Alton Howard (great-grandpa, Mom's side)

MAMAW HOWARD: Jean Howard (great-grandma, Mom's side)

UNCLE SI: Si Robertson (great-uncle, Dad's side)

AUNTS AND UNCLES: Let's just say I have sixteen who live on the same street as me. But that's not all of them! I have even more who live in other places.

SIBLINGS: three sisters (Rebecca, Sadie, and Bella) and two brothers (Will and Rowdy)

FIRST COUSINS: nineteen and counting

SECOND, THIRD, AND SO-ON COUSINS: too many to count

MY TOOLBOX

The story I'm about to tell you was first told to me by 2-Mama, my grandma on my mom's side. I have no memory of it, but I trust her to tell me the truth. She says I was about eight years old and was in the car with her on the way to the grocery store. We had just pulled into the store parking lot when I announced that I had learned three things in life. Apparently, at eight I was quite the philosopher.

"What have you learned?" 2-Mama wanted to know.

I quickly replied, "I've learned that in life you have to work hard, play hard, and expect the unexpected."

2-Mama seemed very impressed, but I wasn't done with my philosophizing.

"Do you know which one is the hardest?" I went on to ask her.

She claims she was all ears by this point, eager to hear words of wisdom from an eight-year-old.

I proclaimed, "The hardest one is expecting the unexpected."

2-Mama has told this story many times. And, I confess, at nineteen years old, as I write this book, I'm amazed at how true those words still are.

Looking back on my nineteen years, I hope I have done what I was philosophizing about.

I think I have worked hard—I've done well in school, spent my summers helping in mission work and summer camps, helped out in the family business, and even started a business of my own.

I know I have played hard—lots of volleyball, card games, tennis matches, hunting trips, and random adventures in the woods.

But what about that last thing I said? *Expecting the unexpected*. I was definitely right about that point being the hardest one.

How can you expect what you don't expect to happen? It seems an impossible task. I think what I meant then, and what I understand now that I'm older and much wiser (☺), is that surprises, opportunities, tragedies, and plot twists (good and bad) are going to happen in life. It's best to just know that up front . . . you should expect the unexpected.

I think my eight-year-old self was on to something, and I think it kind of sums up what I'm hoping to explore in this book. For a little over a year now, I've been on a very personal search to know more about God and what He has planned for my life. It's not that I didn't know God before I started this search; I did. But as you read, you'll see why this past year was my "wake up" year. I've come to understand that God loves to surprise us with the unexpected, and my life journey has been filled with unexpected events. I am honored that you are reading this book and are willing to be a part of my unexpected journeys, but more importantly, I want to challenge you to be alert and ready to "expect the unexpected" in your life too.

The title of my book is *Young and Beardless* for two very good reasons. I am young, and I am beardless. All that really means is I'm still learning and growing and figuring out my life's purpose. I guess I could grow a beard, but I'm pretty sure it would be a little sparse and not very impressive at this point in my life. But the growth potential of my beard isn't important; the growth potential of my life is. Right now, my life might also be a little sparse and unimpressive, but the journey is just beginning. God's not done with me yet.

I have to be honest: it would be easy for me to grow content and complacent with my life because I have been blessed with an amazing family who is quite accomplished and loves me just as I am. If I never accomplished one of my dreams, they will love me just the same. It saddens me that this isn't true for everyone. Having love and support from my family has been "normal" for me, but my wife, Mary Kate, warns, "Never let normal become ungrateful." I will add onto that and say, "Never let normal become uneventful."

Eventually we all have to get out on our own. We can't rely on the faith of our family to get us through life. We have to find it for ourselves. This is what will happen for all of us. We all have to reach the point where we build our own lives and follow the unique path God has set out for us.

Getting on that path can be risky, and you'll want to be prepared for challenges that come your way. Part of being prepared is having the right kind of tools for the job. You can't sweep the floor without a broom, right? So, seven years ago, I started to build my "toolbox for life" when a wise mentor told me to write down everything I find inspiring and put it in a box. He said the box would be my "spiritual toolbox." And I took his advice.

In my spiritual toolbox, I have notes on almost every sermon I have ever heard, notes on almost every book I have ever read, prayers I have prayed, sayings I have heard, thoughts I've had, letters of encouragement from others, and dreams I want to see become reality. Everything. E V E R Y T H I N G. It's all in a massive, expandable file folder labeled "John Luke's Toolbox." It has shaped who I am, and it reminds me to stay focused on the right things. It's not only my toolbox—it's also my personal arsenal.

Why do I choose the word *arsenal*?

My father has one of those walk-in vaults that holds rifles, guns, and crossbows. These are tools for hunting, which my family does often, and these tools make the job a lot easier. From the earliest of days, man has hunted in order to eat. There are museums filled with weapons that people have hunted with for their survival. My spiritual toolbox is a lot like this. The words in it are the weapons I'm going to need for the rest of my life for my spiritual survival.

My toolbox is always there to remind me of who I am and who God wants me to be. I hope that as you read, you'll be inspired to build a toolbox of your own and to fill it with wisdom that will guide you through your life journey. The file folder is my toolbox, but there are other tools that have been valuable to me. There are people who've encouraged me, songs that have inspired me, and events that have challenged me. I know this is the same for you too. Never forget the things that move you to a greater vision for yourself. I think this is the part my younger self philosophized as "work hard." Working hard includes paying attention to the things around you that'll help you grow.

So what caused me to start thinking more deeply about my life? It was a little over a year ago, at summer camp, when a pastor asked this question: *"What do you want to do with your life?"*

I'm sure I had heard this question before, but on that particular day, the question struck me in a different way. I remember writing in my journal later that day and trying to sort out my answers. It was a day of self-discovery as I thought of how God had blessed me with a great family, and we were content right where we were—living life as a family who built duck calls, working in our local church, and loving each other. Then God surprised us with the most unexpected thing: a reality show called *Duck Dynasty*.

That day at camp, writing in my journal, I thought about how much in my family's life had changed; yet in many ways, our entire family had remained the same. My parents and grandparents, Papaw Phil and Mamaw Kay, were now famous, but they were still the same loving couples I grew up with. My aunts and uncles might be on the cover of *Us Weekly* magazine, but they were also at church every Sunday and celebrating family birthdays like they always did. But despite the normal rituals, a big part of our lives had changed forever. It was like each of us had been handed an envelope with the word *opportunities* on it, so I wrote down the following words:

What do I do with this?

Suddenly I realized that *I* had choices to make. And not because of *Duck Dynasty*, or because I was the son of Willie Robertson or the grandson of Phil Robertson, but because I was the son of a living God—who, in His wisdom, handed me an envelope that was labeled *opportunities*.

Think for a minute about your life. No matter what has happened—good times, hard times, fun, tragedy, everything—you, too, have an envelope with the word *opportunities* written on it. God tells us so in His Word. Luke 11:9 says, "So I say to you: Ask and it will be given to you; seek and you will find; knock and the door will be opened to you" (NIV). Opportunities are open doors that give meaning and purpose to life. Like the door to any home, open doors are there for us to walk through. Sometimes it's hard for us to see those doors. We are blinded by thoughts of "If only . . ."

If only I had more money.

If only I were more athletic.

If only I had time to do the things I want.

If only I had a girlfriend.

I don't care what you have in life: being stuck in the "if onlys" will paralyze you. I want you to scrap the "if onlys" and start thinking a new phrase: "What if?"

What if I had faith as small as a mustard seed?

What if I truly believed that God, the Creator of the Universe, loves me and is living in me?

What if I didn't live with a spirit of fear but with one of power?

You are in the same position I was in at camp that summer. No matter what your experiences have been, it's time for you to ask yourself: *What do I want to do with my life? What do I do with what I have been given?*

For me, in that moment at camp, I felt like God was wrapping His arms around me and holding me up. It was like I had a wave of potential inside me—not because I felt important or super-talented or anything, but because I could hear Philippians 4:13 in my head: "For I can do everything through Christ, who gives me strength."

I knew that I had everything I needed. I had that strength inside. It was like what the Wizard said to the Cowardly Lion, the Tin Man, and the Scarecrow at the end of *The Wizard of Oz*: "Everything you were looking for was right there with you all along." It was like I was saying to myself, *Don't sell yourself short, John Luke. You're young (and beardless), but there's work to be done. And you have everything you need to make it happen.*

Then a different kind of wave hit me. You've been hit by this wave too—I'm sure of it. It's the "doubt" wave. I started thinking about finishing high school and getting married and making major decisions on college and life after college. I felt my brave "you can do it" attitude start to slide off my journaling paper.

But then the pastor finished his talk by encouraging us to pick a verse for our lives, one that represented where we're going. So I picked Ephesians 1:18. "I pray that the eyes of your heart may be enlightened in order that you may know the hope to which he has called you, the riches of his glorious inheritance in his holy people" (NIV).

Looking at this verse, I realized that part of my "inheritance" *is* the things I had gathered up in my toolbox—the things I could use to guide me. I'd like to share some of these tools with you and help you find the tools you have too. They've been right there with you all along.

I hope you believe that God has great things in store for you. I want to empower you to look for those things, to get up and go do them. Being young and beardless is more than a lack of life experience or facial hair. It's about learning, growing, and trying to figure out where you fit in the world. And being able to do great things has nothing to do with where you are in life, what your past is, which family you were born into, or how small your town is. It has to do with your faith in the great and loving God that you serve. It has to do with *you*: who you choose to be, how you choose to live, what you choose to dream, and how you choose to get there.

You can become the person you want to be.

So start gathering your tools, and get *started*.

PART 1

WHO AM I?

Examine yourselves, to see whether you
are in the faith. Test yourselves. Or do
you not realize this about yourselves,
that Jesus Christ is in you?—unless
indeed you fail to meet the test!

—2 CORINTHIANS 13:5 ESV

CHAPTER 1

KNOWING

(MYSELF)

> Imagine yourself as a living house. God
> comes in to rebuild that house. . . . You
> thought you were being made into a decent
> little cottage: but He is building a palace.
> He intends to come and live in it Himself.
>
> —C. S. LEWIS

SO I'VE GOT THIS FAMILY . . .

Who we are is largely defined by the family we are born into. Have you ever thought how different your life would be if you weren't born in the twentieth or twenty-first century? Or if you didn't have your particular parents, or live in your particular town? I have. When I was thirteen, I traveled to England with Mamaw Jo to visit my 2-Mama and 2-Papa. They were living in Oxford, England, for one semester as guests of a professor at Oxford University. This worked out pretty great for me because I got to see England at a young age.

We visited castles and prisons, and even where some of *Harry Potter* was filmed. At one castle, we got to fight with fake swords and play games they had in medieval times. I imagined myself as a little boy with no TV or cell phone. I thought how different my life would be if my parents were king and queen, or if my dad were a prison guard and my mom a maid in the fifteenth century. There, surrounded by castle walls that were dark and dingy with age, in a country that is centuries older than America, it was easy to let my imagination run wild and picture a different life.

But that's not the life I've had. I was born in 1995 to Korie and Willie Robertson in West Monroe, Louisiana. I was my parents' firstborn and the first grandchild born on my mom's side of the family, so that honor came with all the attention you would expect a firstborn to get. I have a lot of baby photos that feature me—with about ten pairs of hands touching me. From the beginning, I'm happy to say I was loved.

My life journey is my own and no one else's. It is the same for you too. One famous king in the Bible, King David, captured perfectly how unique our identities are in Psalm 139: "For you formed my inward parts; you knitted me together in my mother's womb. I praise you, for I am fearfully and wonderfully made" (Psalm 139:13–14 ESV).

Understanding that God created you for this very time is critical for knowing your purpose. When we dwell in a life that isn't ours, we are in danger of missing the amazing plans God has for us. When you were born, where you live, whose child you are, where you go to school—all of these details are part of who you are and are part of the life story you are writing. We aren't defined by these details, but God can use them—if we let Him—to shape us for our good and His glory.

Before you start traveling toward a destination, you have to know where you're starting from. The same holds true for life: in order to figure out where you want to go, you first have to know who you are. So . . . who are you? You're not your name, your address, your cell phone number. You're not just your parents' kid, or how many siblings you have. So take a second and think: who you are at your very core?

To help you get started, I'll tell you more of my story.

Who Am I?

Some people are known by one name. Oprah. Jordan. Elvis. Drake.

I'm one of those people who gets to go by two.

My dad was a huge fan of *Star Trek: The Next Generation* back in the day, and it's rumored that Dad liked Captain Jean-Luc Picard so much that he became my namesake. But my grandpa's name is John, and my great-grandpa's name was Luke, so either way, my name comes with good roots.

I'm one of the younger generation on *Duck Dynasty*, and a teen who has become an adult in front of millions. The first episode of the show aired on March 21, 2012, when I was sixteen years old and the show had over 1.8 million viewers.

That's quite a way to introduce yourself to the world.

Since we had been filming long before the first episode aired, my entire high school experience was centered on a reality television show. So many amazing things happened during those years. Our family got to travel to places like Hawaii and attend events, like the Country Music Awards, that would've only been a dream if the show didn't exist. But there are two sides to every coin, and the show didn't come without some challenges.

During my teen years, when most people would rather hide, the country was discovering things about me that even I wasn't aware of. Like how I'm awkward sometimes. Or how I look in the dentist's chair after anesthesia. Or what my dating life was like. Or how many times my father has to say, "John Luke!"

I do have to ask myself this question: if the show hadn't already introduced me to the world, how would I introduce myself? I'm a married man now, so I asked my wife, Mary Kate— the person who knows me best—some things people might not know about me. She said the following:

- He's a dreamer. (Absolutely.)
- He's oblivious to the world around him. (Wait—what world?)
- He's smart. (Good to know. I thought she loved me for my looks!)
- His favorite snack is sourdough bread with olive oil, vinegar, salt, and pepper. (Love it—who doesn't?)
- He reads more books than I thought humanly possible. (And I want to keep reading even more.)
- He hates Doritos. (And the mess they leave on your hands after eating them. Not that I actually eat them.)

I like that Mary Kate said I'm a dreamer and I'm smart. I think both of those traits are a result of another trait she listed—I am a reader. I've spent hours buried in books when I'm sure Mary Kate and others would've preferred I was doing something else.

But I absolutely love reading. I can't ever read *too* much. As I share my life and my story in this book, I want to also share lots of other books that have inspired me. Those books and their authors have had a huge impact on my life. I hope to inspire you to crack open more books on a regular basis. They're an incredible source of wisdom, and one of them might just change your entire outlook on life. One thing's for certain: books have helped define exactly who I am.

In the Infernal Devices series, author Cassandra Clare sums up my view of the written word perfectly: "One must always be careful of books . . . and what is inside them, for words have the power to change us." Maybe this quote is a warning to you as a reader. This book, like any book, should change you. So, if you like where you are, you'd better put it down. But if you're ready to grow, keep flipping the pages!

Who Are You?

Maybe you have never stopped to answer that question. Today's the day to do that.

Because if you don't, the world will.

This world we live in is always trying to define you in the simplest ways possible. Many times, we're defined by the check marks we put on surveys.

Male or Female. *Check one.*

Student or Employed. *Check one.*

USA citizen or Other. *Check one.*

Today's the day to go deeper than the survey. Here are some things you could do to look at yourself in a deeper way:

- Type a sentence describing who you are.
- Look through a magazine and pick different pictures that define you.
- Make a Pinterest board. (Okay, that one's for the ladies reading this book.)
- Connect with other people who have similar tastes and hobbies.
- Create a list of your interests and talents.

Thinking more broadly about your relationships and your interests will help you see what makes up your life, but these are still only parts of you. They're a little like shadows—blurry and one-dimensional portraits of the true you. The goal of this chapter is for you to look at yourself in a deeper way. Aside from what you put on social media or the persona you show to others, you must ask yourself honestly: *Who am I?*

Speaking of Boxes

A check box on a survey isn't the only box that tries to define us. We live in a world full of boxes. We all carry phones shaped like boxes. And those boxes have smaller boxes inside them full of contacts, games, and social networks. We spend hours in front of other boxes, like computer screens and televisions. We drive in square vehicles and head to our square homes outlined with nice, square yards. We sit in square classrooms at school. Every part of our lives fits in a box, and we know how we should act in each box.

Okay, maybe I'm overdoing the whole box thing. But I want you to get a mental picture of the kinds of boxes that shape us. I want you to see that while a box shapes, it also contains and hinders. Boxes can hold out and hold in certain things. While a box is great for wrapping a present or storing your memories, it's not so great if it's hindering or holding back *you*. I want us to look at the boxes that define us.

All of us tend to put people into boxes and slap labels on them. We can't seem to help labeling each other. Of course, many of these labels happen to be very accurate. For instance, when it comes to hobbies, Papaw Phil is put into the "duck hunter" box. And this is very accurate. He doesn't miss a day of duck hunting season. Not a single day. He is defined as a duck hunter. But like everyone else, Papaw Phil is so much more than just that one box.

When it comes to life outlook, people tend to look at Papaw Phil and put him in a box that says he's mean, rough, and intolerant. That box is totally false. Papaw Phil is wise, kind, and loves everyone. I have never heard him say a mean-spirited thing about someone. Don't get me wrong—he has his opinions, but he's never mean-spirited.

Boxes can be dangerous when we force someone into one before we get to know them. Sometimes you think you know somebody, but it turns out you really don't know them at all. We're all guilty of looking at someone and forming instant opinions.

I know that happens to me. People see me in public and call out, "John Luke!" as if they've known me for years. In some ways, they *have* known a part of me for years. They've known the guy they've seen on nine seasons of a reality show.

But that guy on TV is only a small part of who I am—a kid

growing up in the Robertson family. Sometimes goofy and sometimes trying to figure out what to say. Those things are true,
though they aren't the whole picture.

We seldom show others our whole selves. Thankfully, God
sees that whole picture, and He also can see that each one of us
is unique. God doesn't see boxes. He sees beautiful and broken
souls made in His image—all diverse, yet all needing Him at the
same time.

Being on a television show has helped me figure out who I
really am. I can turn on the TV and watch me in a particular
episode, yet deep down I know that's only one side of me. I am
not multiple people in different boxes; I am one person who has
to live in different boxes. I bet you know what I'm talking about.
Life gets difficult when we try to act like something we are not.
When we try to fit into a box by being a personality we think
others want to see, we rob ourselves of being confident in who
we really are.

Now, I don't want you to confuse acting a certain way with
behaving appropriately. Of course we don't behave in school the
same way we behave at a football game. I'm not talking about
that. I'm talking about acting like we are different people in our
different boxes: school, work, home, church. I've done it. But
after acting like different people in each of those boxes, I started
to feel like my life was in pieces. It was awkward when someone
who knew me from one box saw me in another box. Sometimes
I could tell they were disappointed in what they saw. It hurts
when you know someone realizes you aren't who they thought
you were. Eventually I figured out that being the same person in
all my boxes made me feel a lot better. Once I figured that out, I
became more comfortable with myself.

The same could be said for you. There are all sorts of ways others see you—someone's child, a sibling, a friend, your Instagram persona. But that's just a small part of who you are. Deep down, there's only one real you—the person God has a unique plan for. You're extraordinary and unusual in the best ways. Don't let one box define you.

All through school, I searched for a sport that I could play well. Baseball (struck out every time and quit), football (fractured my shoulder and had to quit), even golf (broke a club and was asked to quit)—they were all challenging for me. "Sports" is a box the world likes to put around people. With the amount of money athletes make, the message is loud and clear: if you can hit a home run, dunk a basketball, or throw a spiral, you can do anything. Well, the truth is, not all of us can do that—in fact, very few of us can. Once I decided that I wasn't going to let the world define me by my athletic ability, I was one step closer to becoming the man God wants me to become.

You see, we humans do this to each other constantly. We put our friend in a box, and we keep them there with our expectations—and our words. Think about it. Even the guy who is good at baseball might not want to be a baseball player, yet we keep pushing him toward that goal. Or we use words like, "She's a worrier" or "He just doesn't like to get up in front of the class" to define our friends or family members. We don't even stop to think how those simple words put a box around people we love.

So how do you live outside the boxes the world puts you in? How do you find a dream and make that dream a reality? I think you start by celebrating where you came from and who God made you to be. The "who God made you to be" part will have a lot to do with getting to know yourself, pinpointing your dream, and following your God-given passions in life. We'll talk more about this later. But no one knows where you've come from better than you. Your story is a gift only you can use.

Now let me tell you a little more of my story.

Out of Nowhere

My life, which seems very normal to me, is apparently not so normal. Since the TV show first aired, I became aware that most people had never heard of a duck call, let alone a Duck Commander duck call. On top of that, most people didn't know a family in northeast Louisiana could build a business by selling lots and lots of duck calls. And that family could all work together, have fun doing it, and grow really long beards.

The public soon learned such a family existed, and we lived in a city called West Monroe, Louisiana. Again, that raised more questions. Where in the world is West Monroe? Who is from West Monroe? Some might have seen bits and pieces of Louisiana in movies. Perhaps they'd visited New Orleans, or watched their favorite football team play in the Superdome, or seen the movie *Steel Magnolias*. Maybe everything they knew about the state came from watching the news about Hurricane Katrina. But a business called Duck Commander, in backwoods Louisiana? Prior to the airing of our first *Duck Dynasty* show, it was only known to diehard hunters.

"Is this place for real?" was the question asked in many living rooms in America.

It's very real, and it's the only place I've ever called home.

While West Monroe might seem like it's in the middle of

nowhere, good things can and do come out of nowhere. All the time. I'll give you a couple of examples

Your hometown might have a run-of-the-mill airport, but ours has an interesting history. During World War II, more than fifteen thousand pilots were trained on the grounds where our airport now sits. Built near Monroe in 1942, the airport was called Selman Army Airfield and was the only full navigation training station in the country during the war. Navigators trained at Selman flew in every WWII fighting region.

And then there is the true story of an African American boy born into the totally segregated town of West Monroe in 1934. His family struggled and eventually headed west in hopes of a better future. Times continued to be tough for his family and at age twelve, the boy lost his mother. He didn't seem particularly gifted in any way, and his future didn't seem so bright. Yet this boy ended up becoming one of the greatest athletes of all time. His name is Bill Russell. He won eleven NBA championships in thirteen years with the Boston Celtics. Get this—Russell won an NCAA championship, an Olympic gold medal, and an NBA title *in the same year.*

Russell said the following about his life and where he came from:

> I hope I epitomize the American dream. For I came against long odds, from the ghetto to the very top of my profession. I was not immediately good at basketball. It did not come easy. It came as the result of a lot of hard work and self-sacrifice. The rewards, where [*sic*] they worth it? One thousand times over.

It doesn't matter where you come from, how the world defines you, or what life seems to have in store for you. Dreaming is a gift given to each of us. From the pilots who trained to serve our country to every young person with a difficult beginning like Bill Russell's, dreams can and do come true to those who work hard to make them happen.

With God's help, you can and should dream big. Then work hard to see what happens with those dreams.

Lost and Found

There's a popular song called "Wake Me Up" by an artist named Avicii. A line from the chorus talks about trying to find yourself when you didn't even realize you were lost. (I've been told I can't quote song lyrics because of some kind of law, so you can look it up on Google.) This song speaks to so many young people today. Some of us spend our entire youth trying to find ourselves— never realizing what we're missing, never quite knowing how lost we might actually be.

The lyrics remind me of a line from one of those life-changing books I read. A few years ago, I read *The 7 Habits of Highly Effective Teens* by Sean Covey. It's the teen version of the bestselling book *The 7 Habits of Highly Effective People*, which was written by his father, Stephen Covey. Early on in the book, Sean Covey shares a great quote: "If who I am is what I have and what I have is lost, then who am I?"[1]

The quote was not attributed to anyone, but a Google search turned up a quote from a German psychoanalyst named Erich Fromm, who originally said, "If I am what I have and what I have is lost, who then am I?"[2]

Okay, that's deep stuff, right? I know—a few pages into my book, and I'm quoting German psychoanalysts. That's what being a reader will get you—quotes by really smart people. To put it simply, Fromm is asking this: if you lose all the things you think you are . . . then who are you?

What if I were no longer a Robertson? What if I no longer lived in West Monroe, Louisiana? What if I couldn't go to Liberty University, or be married to Mary Kate, or be called by my first two names? Do all those things define me?

I know they don't. I know that all of my experiences are parts of me and have contributed to who I am, but they don't define me. If I strip those experiences away, I'm still me. Where does this confidence come from? God is the only one who can truly *define me.* And He is the only one who can truly define *you.*

Jesus defined Himself in John 8:12 by saying, "I am the light of the world. If you follow me, you won't have to walk in darkness, because you will have the light that leads to life."

Jesus is my light, and I'm so grateful that He is. When things start to get confusing and there seems to be so much darkness in this world, I have a Light to guide me who never changes or burns out. Hebrews 13:8 tells us that Jesus "is the same yesterday, today, and forever." That's awesome to me. Jesus' life on earth, His death for me and you, and His resurrection continue to be my guiding light.

I'm glad that even while I continue trying to find myself in this world, I know I'm *not* lost. I know I'm *not* alone and undefined. I'm following the light that leads to life. Jesus knew who He was and told others. He knew what He was meant to do.

I believe God can reveal to us who He wants us to be too. He promises, "Trust in the LORD with all your heart, and do not lean on your own understanding. In all your ways acknowledge him, and he will make straight your paths" (Proverbs 3:5–6 ESV).

If you're a normal person, you rushed through that verse, but read it again. Trust in who? Acknowledge who? Do not lean on what? Who will make your paths straight? These are all important questions that this verse answers. Here's the bottom line: follow God, and He'll get us where we need to go.

In or Out

I grew up in a Christian family. Mom and Dad taught us what Christ meant to them and how He needed to be the center of our lives. They had committed themselves to Christ when they were teens, so it was natural for my dad to talk to me about my relationship with Jesus. I was twelve when Dad took me aside and had a conversation about faith.

"Look, son," he told me. "One day you're going to have to decide whether you're going to follow God or not."

I nodded, knowing what he was talking about as well as any twelve-year-old could. But then he gave me advice that I still think about every day of my life:

So, John Luke, you're either hot or cold. If you're in, then you go 100 percent, all the way with Christ. If you're not, then you go 100 percent the other way. But listen. If you're in the middle, then you'll be miserable. You can either have joy— the pure joy that only comes from God—or you can have the empty pleasure that this world offers. But for those in the middle, they have neither.

Not long after this, I began to understand my dad's point: I had to start committing myself to God in all areas. Living in the middle was starting to get uncomfortable. My best friend, Taylor Mayfield, and I decided to make a pact. We had discovered this thing called the Internet and realized how many temptations waited for us on it. We both knew we needed help to keep our thoughts in line. And we realized if we asked God for help, then the right actions would follow. The struggle we were dealing with could *only* be conquered by having God on our side. Together, we promised to help each other stay strong and pure and not let the evil one enter our lives through our computers.

When I was fourteen years old, I committed my life to Christ. This meant acknowledging my faults and my weaknesses. It meant realizing Jesus was my Lord and Savior. It meant allowing God to finally have my back in whatever big or small struggle I might encounter.

Papaw Phil baptized me in the river, just as he had baptized my father, my three uncles, and many others. My friends and my family surrounded me as I was dipped in the dirty Ouachita River.

I didn't find myself when I was fourteen. I was fourteen when I finally found my Savior. That has to be the first step toward the future, and it's the most important one. That dirty water made me clean and whole. Without God, we can't get anywhere. With Him, anything is possible.

So while you're asking "Who am I?" and "What will I be?" know that there are some things you can count on right now if you're with God. If you're God's child, the Bible makes it clear exactly who you are—not who you will be or who you might be one day if you shape up, but who you *are* if you know Him as Savior. Here are some things the Bible says you are:

- free (John 8:36)
- holy (1 Corinthians 6:19)
- strong (Philippians 4:13)
- heading toward something good (Philippians 1:6)
- not condemned (Romans 8:1)
- not fearful or timid, but powerful, loving, and self-disciplined (2 Timothy 1:7)
- confident against any opposition (Romans 8:31)

And all these things are possible because Christ lives in you (Galatians 2:20).[3]

Don't Just Settle

Around the same time as I was committing my life to God, I met my soul mate, Mary Kate. One summer, instead of attending the camp I had always attended, I decided to try something new. So I skipped my beloved Camp Ch-Yo-Ca, and I went to another summer camp called Kings Camp. It was there that I met Mary Kate. Later I found out this was the camp *she* went to every summer. (Side note: I'm a strong believer in Christian camps. If you haven't been to one, go. Go without any preconceived ideas, and let God work.)

One day Mary Kate and I were placed on the same team for a wall-sit competition. You know, wall-sits: you lean against a wall and bend your legs into a sitting position, and your legs feel like they're on fire within five seconds. The goal is to see who can last the longest. Having Mary Kate there distracted me from the pain in my legs and my back. We talked about a lot of things during the contest—how she lived an hour away from my hometown, what her family was like, all the different connections we had.

I knew I liked this girl after getting to know a little about her. I can't remember who won the contest, but I do know Mary Kate had won my heart. (Kind of corny, I know, but true.)

Then two years went by, and we didn't even talk. It was one of those brief encounters with somebody when you give them a little insight into your soul, and then they're gone. Sometimes you never see them again.

Fortunately, I did see Mary Kate again (more on that in another chapter). When I finally got to know this girl and her family, I could tell right away that she knew who she was. Mary Kate not only shared the same faith I had in Christ, but she also had a strength I had not seen in other girls her age. She also came from a strong Christian family, which I admired.

Mary Kate's father told her then, and still tells her, that she is a daughter of the King, and because of that she deserves the best. She is worthy of everything God has to give her. Her father once taught a Sunday school class he titled "God Leaves the Best for Those Who Leave the Choices with Him," based on a quote by Jim Elliot. This was how Mary Kate chose to live her life growing up.

It's also how she chose to view dating—something Mary Kate had never done until meeting me.

While so many of her friends had boyfriends, and while the culture around her made the whole dating thing seem like something natural and even necessary, Mary Kate remained single. She had made a deal with God regarding dating. "I'm not going to settle for anything less than what You have for me, Lord," she prayed.

She has said that she felt incredibly close to God during her teenage years and depended on Him in many areas of her life. And she discovered that God was faithful to her, so she was faithful to Him.

This was the young woman I became friends with and then fell in love with. How could I *not* love someone with that kind of steadfast faith?

Mary Kate knew she was beautiful and worthy in God's eyes; she didn't need a boy coming along to try to show her that. But a boy came along regardless, and he continues to remind her of those two things every day.

I'm so glad she didn't sell herself short.

I want to give you the same advice Mary Kate's dad gave her: don't settle. Don't ever settle for less than God intends for your life. Isaiah 30:18 says it better than I can say it: "Yet the LORD longs to be gracious to you; therefore he will rise up to show you compassion. For the LORD is a God of justice. Blessed are all who wait for him!" (NIV).

Wow! Think about that verse. The Lord *longs*, which means "eagerly waits," to be good to you. God is just waiting to make your day amazing.

The Point

This chapter is about knowing who you are—knowing how you're defined. And to do that, it's good to know where you're from and where you want to go. But you have to remember what matters most:

- You are definitely known.
- You are definitely worthy.

- And you are asked to be 100 percent in—aka 100 percent on fire.
- You don't have to have a plan. You just have to say yes to the plan God has for you.

This is where I hope you can start.

Like so many others, my life was impacted by Francis Chan's bestselling book *Crazy Love*. Chan describes a model of what the church should look like—a model of love. Not only that—Chan helps us define what the goal of our lives should be: "The point of your life is to point to Him. Whatever you are doing, God wants to be glorified, because this whole thing is His."[4]

So who am I? What's the point of my life? Who, exactly, is John Luke?

Yes, I'm a son of a duck hunter. Yes, I'm young and beardless. Yes, I'm nineteen and married. Yes, I'm not much of a baseball player. Yes, I read and dream and hate Doritos. But much more than all those things, I'm a son of my heavenly Father.

All my hopes and aspirations and desires need to point to Him.

This is the starting point.

This is the kind of line you want in your bio.

THINK ABOUT IT

One of the most important tools in any spiritual toolbox is a journal. It helps me sort out everything going on in my head and really learn the lessons that come my way. (Otherwise they'd be in one ear and out the other. I have to force them to sink in!) So get a journal. And use it. You won't regret it.

Here are a few questions that'll help you find some of the tools in your spiritual toolbox:

1. Go to someone who knows you really well, and ask that person to make a list of things other people might not know about you (like Mary Kate did for me). Once you've read over them, did anything surprise you about that list?

2. What's the biggest difference between the person others see and the person you really are?

3. Is there any difference between the person others say you are and the person God says you are? (See John 1:12; Romans 8:1; Galatians 4:7; Ephesians 1:4.)

4. Are there strong Christian role models in your life, or even some people with successful marriages? Jot down their names, and see if you can sit down and talk with them this week. Tell them what you admire about them, and ask them how they got that way.

5. In your journal, write "Who I Am?" at the top of the page. Sketch out a few bullet points outlining where you come from, who your parents are, and how you've

grown up. You could even make a family tree. Now ask yourself (and God), *What do I do with all this?*

6. Think back to the section on being "100 percent in" or "100 percent out." Where are you on the percentage scale? Are you "on fire," "miserable," or "out"?

After each chapter I'd like to feature a book that has meant a lot to me. I hope you get a chance to read these books and love them as much as I do. You'll find wisdom in everything from fiction to biographies, to books on business, religion, current issues, and beyond. Consider adding them to your toolbox too. I realize that not everyone loves to read as much as I do, but consider giving it a try. You might surprise yourself.

Book Highlight #1:

The 7 Habits of Highly Effective Teens by Sean Covey

Without The 7 Habits of Highly Effective Teens, I would be careless, worn out, and unorganized.

When I read *The 7 Habits of Highly Effective Teens*, I basically wrote half of the book down in a journal. There are so many great quotes inside, like this:

> If you decide to just go with the flow, you'll end up where the flow goes, which is usually downhill, often leading to a big pile of sludge and a life of unhappiness. You'll end up doing what everyone else is doing.[5]

That's the truth. If there's a book outside of the Bible that you can refer to all the time, it's this one. It basically outlines what you need to do in order to be effective. Not only that, but it's also full of great quotes, illustrations, and even action steps to take.

This book is based on the hugely successful, classic leadership book *The 7 Habits of Highly Effective People*, which was written by Sean's father, Stephen Covey. As Sean adapts the bestseller for teens, we find out just how important these habits can be to us at this critical point in our lives.

Here is a list of those seven habits and what they mean:

- Habit 1: Be proactive. (Take responsibility for your life.)
- Habit 2: Begin with the end in mind. (Define your mission and goals.)
- Habit 3: Put first things first. (Prioritize, and do the most important things first.)
- Habit 4: Think win-win. (Have an everyone-can-win attitude.)
- Habit 5: Seek first to understand, then to be understood. (Be teachable.)
- Habit 6: Synergize. (Work together to achieve more.)
- Habit 7: Sharpen the saw. (Renew yourself regularly.)

You know you want to find out more about this. Check out the book, and read an entire chapter on each habit. Nothing will pump you up about your future like knowing you've got the tools to tackle it. These habits will set you on the right path toward future domination (not world domination, but dominating your *own* future).

CHAPTER 2

DREAMING

(BIG)

At the very heart of life there is a song. No
one can sing my song like me. No one can
sing your song like you. What is so special
is that each of us has our own song.

—ALTON H. HOWARD

SO I HAD A DREAM . . .

When I was young I wanted to be Steve Irwin, the Crocodile Hunter. He was the coolest guy I'd ever seen. Maybe it was the Australian accent. Or maybe it was just the fact that he was on television grabbing an inland taipan snake by its tail and then twirling it in front of himself while describing just how deadly it was.

"He has enough venom in one bite to kill a hundred blokes my size!" he would say way too enthusiastically. I watched in awe.

I once heard that Irwin wrestled his first crocodile when he was nine years old. *Nine.* I seriously thought I could do the same when I was going through my Steve Irwin phase.

My dream of becoming Steve Irwin lasted between the ages of seven and nine. I would watch him playing with crocodiles and other animals, and then I would go outside to catch snakes and frogs.

Once I had a Crocodile Hunter birthday party. My dad dressed up like Steve Irwin and brought an actual live alligator to the party. I know. Some dads might be content to simply dress up like the Crocodile Hunter and carry around a stuffed animal, but not mine. No, sir. (Of course, the alligator did have its mouth taped shut. But that didn't matter to me. I thought my dad was as brave as Steve Irwin.)

Like the rest of the world, I was heartbroken when I heard that Steve Irwin had died in a freak accident when he was struck by a stingray in 2006. He was only forty-four years old.

Irwin had pursued and lived out his dreams his entire life. He always said he'd risk his life (and often did) trying to save an animal. He surely saved the lives of countless people as he taught them how to treat snakebites and dangerous animals.

I love this Irwin quote: "Whatever you want to do in this world, it is achievable. The most important thing I've found, that perhaps you could use, is to be passionate and enthusiastic in the direction you choose in life, and you'll be a winner."[1]

All of us have dreams growing up. These can, and often do, change as we grow older. But don't let growing up stop you from dreaming altogether. I'm not very old, but I know that as time goes by, plans get altered. Sometimes thing happen that we don't have control of, and we lose sight of a dream. The tricky part is knowing when to let go of a dream—like my Crocodile Hunter dream—or to hold on to it with all your might. Hopefully, as we work together through this book, some of this will become clearer to you.

Think Differently

Mary Kate and I recently saw the Pixar film *Inside Out*, and we loved it. It really captures what it's like to be human. There's a brilliant sort of creativity at work in every one of Pixar's films. But did you know that Pixar began with the help of one very famous guy who has likely changed your life? If you've owned an iPhone, worked on a Mac, or played on an iPad, you probably know who I'm talking about.

Steve Jobs.

He was a visionary dreamer who dropped out of college to search for himself and his purpose. He was endlessly curious. His career is fascinating, especially because he started Apple Computer at only twenty-one years old, and then became a millionaire and a celebrity. Yet, by the time he was thirty, Jobs had been fired by the same company he'd built.

In the years after, Steve Jobs spent his time exploring opportunities and working on other business ventures. He ended up with a controlling interest in the computer graphics division of George Lucas's company, Lucasfilm. This small, independent company with fewer than fifty employees would become Pixar.

Ultimately Jobs went back to Apple in 1997, where he was tasked to rebuild a company in decline. To do that, he started to dream again. And he shared those dreams in a very public and proud way, with a now-famous marketing campaign called

"Think Different." These are the words of Apple's iconic television ad:

> Here's to the crazy ones. The misfits. The rebels. The troublemakers. The round pegs in the square holes. The ones who see things differently. They're not fond of rules. And they have no respect for the status quo. You can quote them, disagree with them, glorify or vilify them. About the only thing you can't do is ignore them. Because they change things. They push the human race forward. And while some may see them as the crazy ones, we see genius. Because the people who are crazy enough to think they can change the world, are the ones who do.[2]

Jobs and his team followed those statements by changing the world with technology. The iMac, the iPod, the iPhone—it's hard to imagine a world without them.

Visionaries tend to see things differently, and they're crazy enough to think they can change the world. They aren't content to be put in a box. I like to think I'm one of those crazy round pegs in a square hole. And you might see yourself that way too.

But it doesn't matter what category you are in. Everyone has dreams; you have to start with believing that your dreams are important and can make an impact. Once you do that, you can start making a plan.

The History of Your Future

Picture yourself ten years from now.

No, really. If it helps, close your eyes. Take a break from reading, and imagine yourself ten years from now.

One of our family friends, Rick Krug, came to West Monroe to give me a crash course in public speaking. He told me that the best definition for a vision is having a highly detailed mental picture of a preferable future. That's kind of a wordy definition, but it just means this—being able to picture yourself in the future.

When you imagine yourself ten years in the future, don't just stop at imagining what life might be like in general. Picture the job you have. Imagine the house you're living in. Envision your spouse greeting you as you open the front door. Hear the screams of your children as they rush toward you. Listen to the way you describe your day at your job.

Who are you, and what are you doing?

I tried this experiment in 2014 when I was eighteen years old. I pictured myself at twenty-eight. I pictured where I wanted to be—the place where my big, outrageous, and impossible dreams would take me.

Once you start to picture what your life looks like in ten years, there's a very important question you'll have to ask: *Which decision did you make ten years ago that got you off on the right foot?*

When Rick had me do this exercise, it was revolutionary. Right away I began to write down my objectives, desires, and expectations. I made lists of what I wanted, what I hoped for, the things I could do. I then backtracked and figured out what my action steps needed to be. I prayed that God would allow these things to start happening.

You never know what today, much less tomorrow, might bring. Life became a whirlwind just as I entered high school. My high school years didn't happen as I originally planned *at all*. It's been a crazy, exciting, and life-changing journey.

What crazy, exciting, life-changing events have happened on your journey? Don't worry—it doesn't have to be a TV show to be a life-changer. I've had plenty of other things change my course: when my family moved, when I broke up with my first girlfriend, when I broke my collarbone in football, and when I met a young man from Australia (more on this later). Life-altering events happen every day. Don't ignore them. Look for them. Celebrate them.

Passion and Faith

I can't imagine what sort of dreams Alton Howard might have had during his childhood growing up on a small cotton farm in Rocky Branch, Louisiana. Alton Howard was my great-grandfather. We called him Papaw Howard. He spent entire summers of his childhood picking cotton, just to pay for his overalls and shoes for the next school year. I can imagine him dreaming of better days while standing, day after day, in the hot Louisiana sun. I don't know what his dreams were, but I do know what he became. And I know his family had a powerful faith in God that bound them together and gave them the hope they had for a better tomorrow.

When people reach the end of their life, it's hard to imagine them as young kids or teens. I was fortunate to live across the street from Papaw Howard in his later years, and I'm in awe of all he accomplished. Papaw Howard served in the Ninth Air Force in World War II as a gunner on a B-26 bomber. After coming home from war, he married Jean Meador, my Mamaw Howard. Then he and his brother developed and opened a variety of businesses, including a chain of discount stores. After selling those, he and my grandfather, John Howard (2-Papa), and other family members opened a chain of warehouse clubs called SuperSaver Wholesale Warehouse Club. They later sold those stores to Sam Walton, and they became part of the Sam's Club chain. While Papaw Howard loved business, one of his greatest loves was music. Out of this love came another dream.

Dreams often start in simple places. They're often born out of joy and hope. For Papaw Howard, it was the simple love of singing and writing hymns that fostered his dream of having his songs published. This was the reason he eventually founded Howard Publishing in 1969. It was a small publishing company with the sole purpose of printing a hymnal that would have the great songs of the church, plus Papaw Howard's own songs.

Living across the street allowed me to watch Papaw Howard play the piano, work on his next songbook, follow the stock market, and discuss business with his son, 2-Papa. Papaw Howard always seemed to wear three or four hats at a time, even if he never got out of his pajamas. By the time I was born, he had been retired for many years and sometimes stayed in his pajamas all day. Yet he was always working on a project.

His first hymnal was one of these projects. For a long time it was the only book Howard Publishing had, but that one book was pretty successful. From Papaw Howard's garage, three million hymnals were sold! (Trust me, I thought the singing and piano thing might be a good life choice for myself, but so far it looks like that gene didn't get handed down to me.)

Papaw Howard's love of singing and making music came from a deeper love: the one he had for the Lord. My great-grandfather's successes were poured back into a variety of ministries and used to further the kingdom of Christ—just as when he created the Christian youth camp called Camp Ch-Yo-Ca in 1967.

Camp Ch-Yo-Ca is where my grandparents, John and Chrys Howard, met. It's also where my mom and dad met when they were in the third grade. And it's where my father began working in 1995 after my parents were married. To top it off, Camp Ch-Yo-Ca has also been one of the biggest influencers of my life.

When a dream starts from the right place, God will surely bless it. For my great-grandfather, he simply loved his Lord and wanted to serve Him however he could. So much of the Howard and Robertson families was knit together by the passion and faith of Alton Howard. He grabbed hold of his dreams, working hard to bring them to life, and his effort created blessings for multiple generations.

I read a blog called *Song Scoops* about my Papaw Howard. The writer wondered what the secret was to Papaw's "life-song" and the joy and exuberance that was found in his life and his writing. The blogger suggested that Papaw's willingness to take risks was perhaps because he knew God "had his back," and his confidence came from the knowledge that all of a Christian's adventures would lead back to God. I hope someone can say that about my life one day.

Announce It

"I'm going to sell a million dollars' worth of duck calls," Papaw Phil announced to his family one day.

If you know anything about us, you know how the duck call business turned out. The thing I take away from Papaw Phil's story is his unwavering confidence. It wasn't arrogance or being ridiculous. He wasn't like somebody who had never played football waking up one day and declaring that he was going to be a starting quarterback in the NFL. Papaw Phil's belief in his success was based on turning a dream into solid plan and going for it. At the time he didn't have any money, the equipment needed to make the calls, or a sales team to promote the duck calls. He only had a dream.

Papaw Phil's idea to start Duck Commander began with his hunting friend, Al Bolen. One day Al told Papaw Phil that he wasn't just calling ducks with Papaw Phil's duck call invention; he was *commanding* them. Papaw Phil wanted to build and sell the best duck calls in the world, yet initially all he had was that dream. He had to look down the road and take a mental picture of what his future as the Duck Commander could look like. And like Alton Howard, Phil Robertson discovered his why—to build the best duck call ever—announced it, and then began to work toward the future.

What's the significance of announcing a dream? Putting words to something turns it from a vague idea to a concrete action. It turns our words from being disorganized thoughts like, *I'd kinda sorta maybe like to get into the duck call business one day*, into something you can build a plan on.

It also comes with accountability. If your dream is strong enough to make you want to tell the world—to tell others—then you can get support. You can ask others to back you, or ask trusted advisors to tell you what the pitfalls might be. When you announce a dream, you give it a chance to live in a world outside your own head.

The Ice Cabin

Now to one of my dreams. I love Snow-Balls. Some people call them shaved ice, or Sno-Cones, but in Louisiana we call shaved ice with sugary flavoring a Snow-Ball. Since I was young, I dreamed of opening a Snow-Ball stand. Not just a table-on-the-side-of-the-road kind of stand, but a genuine Snow-Ball stand, with a building and everything. I wanted to be a serious competitor in the Snow-Ball world.

So a few years ago, I decided to make it happen. I announced my idea, but it got shot down. It was kind of like my dad said, "One day, maybe, but this is not that day." My parents will say this about me—when I get an idea, I don't easily let it go. I kept trying to convince them that my dream was a good one, and my dad kept trying to convince me that it wasn't. One day I made this declaration:

"This is the year I'm gonna open the Snow-Ball stand."

I guess I had finally said it enough, because on that day, Dad gave me a quick nod and finally said, "Okay. Let's do it together." And by that, he meant he would help with some of the start-up costs, but the work would all be on me. It was a deal I couldn't refuse, and my dream was on its way.

John Luke and Willie's Ice Cabin now proudly stands in front of the Duck Commander warehouse. We just call it the Ice Cabin. We're open from eleven to seven every day except Sunday, and we sell practically every kind of Snow-Ball flavor you can imagine. We're always trying new and adventurous combinations.

It's been a great experience working there with the other employees as we build the business together. The skills I've learned at the Ice Cabin are skills I will use in every area of my life: hiring people, working with others, finding the right equipment, handling breakdowns (equipment *and* employees), choosing flavors, and dealing with customers. Plus, I've been able to hire many of my friends from my youth group and give them opportunities for summer work.

You can and should have dreams to change the world. But at the same time, be patient until the time is right. I had to trust my dad's wisdom (which the Bible calls "wise counsel") and wait for the right time.

And never forget: dreams that change the world aren't always big dreams, and they don't always require money. They can be dreams of seeing your children know more about God. To honor the older people in your community with small deeds. To sing in front of an audience and lead in a worship band. Dreams are yours, and you get to decide how to use them to bring God glory and make the world a better place.

Timing Is Everything

It's one thing to have dreams, to write them down, and even to announce them. But it's another thing to act upon them—and that can be hard. The timing may not always seem right. You may feel like you have to hurry too quickly. You may not be ready to act when the right moment shows up unannounced. Like when I heard from my sister Sadie that her best friend liked me.

As I mentioned, I met Mary Kate at camp before ninth grade, yet it was a couple more years before I even saw her again. As it turned out, she started attending Ouachita Christian School, where my sister and I went. I still remember the moment

I opened the doors to chemistry class and saw Mary Kate standing there. Suddenly a gust of wind swirled around us, her hair started to blow, and a radiant light enveloped her while angels began to sing the "Hallelujah Chorus" . . .

Okay, well, that might not be exactly how it happened, but it sure feels like that to me now.

There certainly was chemistry at the start (and not just because it was chemistry class). I would tell her stories in return for her helping me with my homework. But we didn't start dating right away. Our friendship grew in a variety of ways, especially when we'd drive together to her church. Yet every time I asked her out for a real date, she said no. One time I felt confident enough during one of those car rides to slip my hand into hers. Mary Kate slipped her hand right back out.

The dream could've stopped right there. Especially when she told me point-blank, "It's never going to happen."

But somehow things changed.

A couple of months after the "never going to happen" moment, Sadie told me she got a text from Mary Kate saying that she liked me. The only problem was that I was dating someone else. So I had to have a serious talk with Mary Kate to ask what was going on. Mary Kate didn't hesitate in telling me the truth.

"Look. I know I made a mistake," she said. "I know I missed my shot, John Luke. But I have to tell you this: you're an amazing guy. Whether you choose me or this other girl, I know you're a godly man and will pray about it. I know you'll make the right decision. I trust you. Just know that I wouldn't date a guy I wouldn't marry. And I'd date you."

Boom.

Her words made up my mind right at that moment. Come

on—how could I say no to someone who said something like that?

Of course, I had to play it cool for a while. Almost a year had passed since she had reappeared in my life. Then, after Mary Kate came along with us on a family vacation, we stood together in the kitchen for some straight talk.

"So, what are we doing?" Mary Kate asked. "What exactly is this?"

"Well, if I saw you walking down the road and I was with my friends, I'd say, 'Yeah, that's my girl.'"

Mary Kate gave me a nod. "I can live with that."

Romantic, huh?

I'd like to say that I knew Mary Kate was "The One" the first time I met her at camp years ago. Somewhere deep down, maybe that's true. But life is not like the movies, and there aren't always earth-shattering moments when you know exactly which road to take. It's more like a series of tiny actions and small yeses.

Somehow a little feeling between Mary Kate and me turned into a dream of being together. Both of us chased after this dream at different points in our relationship. But neither of us stood still. God doesn't either. He knew the exact right time for the two of us to finally get together. And suddenly I no longer pictured just myself ten years in the future. I pictured Mary Kate beside me.

Acting on a dream had been scary for both of us. We risked rejection and being humbled. We could've let it pass us by. But looking back, I see how God perfectly timed the opportunities for each of us to step up. I'm so glad we both took action. Finally Mary Kate and I could imagine what our future might bring—together.

Then and Now

Back to you. Can you picture yourself ten years from now?

Name some of the things you'll have accomplished by then. In those ten years, what did you do that led to success?

Now come back to the present. What are the things you need to give up so you can achieve your dream of success? Which habits, relationships, beliefs, and motives should you part with so that you can become who you're meant to be?

Which people, places, hopes, and beliefs should you be striving toward?

When you achieve the relationships and habits you envision, then hold on to them as you live out your future. The history of your future is not set in stone. You will make mistakes and have to change the goals, relationships, and habits that you, at one time, were so sure of. Don't lose faith in the future. You are not alone.

If you let Him, God will help you with your future. Faith in God's help will bring joy, as the Bible says in Romans 5:2–5:

> Because of our faith, Christ has brought us into this place of undeserved privilege where we now stand, and we confidently and joyfully look forward to sharing God's glory.
>
> We can rejoice, too, when we run into problems and trials, for we know that they help us develop endurance. And endurance develops strength of character, and character strengthens our confident hope of salvation. And this hope will not lead to disappointment. For we know how dearly God loves us, because he has given us the Holy Spirit to fill our hearts with his love.

Whatever your ten-year vision might be, give it the attention it needs to happen. Because of God's love and guidance, we know that dreams become reality with endurance, character, and hope in Him. Start by discovering those dreams, and get ready to press on through.

THINK ABOUT IT

1. Write down your ten-year vision in your journal, and circle back to answer the questions I asked in the last part of this chapter:

   • What is your big dream?
   • What did you do ten years ago that led to your success?
   • Which things (habits, relationships, motives, beliefs) do you need to let go of to get there?
   • Which key things (people, places, habits, hopes, beliefs) do you need to strive toward?

2. Papaw Phil and Papaw Howard both found the "why" behind their dreams. What's the "why" behind yours? Why do you want to end up that way, and how can you use that to motivate you?

3. Try putting your dream into one sentence, like Papaw Phil did when he announced that he wanted to sell a million dollars' worth of duck calls. Write it down on a piece of paper.

4. Think about some people you love and trust. Who can you announce your dream to? Give it a try.

5. Think of times when opportunities to take action passed you by. How did that feel? How can you avoid that in the future?

6. Name three small action steps you can take to fulfill your dream (the smaller, the better). Reach out and

grab some this week, and record how it went in your journal.

7. The Bible says we will have failures, and "problems and trials" (Romans 5:3), but that they will help us build endurance. List three times when you've failed or encountered problems on the way toward a dream, and ask God how He will turn those failures into endurance.

Book Highlight #2:

The Hobbit by J. R. R. Tolkien

Without The Hobbit, *I would still be shut in my room without an adventure to share.*

J. R. R. Tolkien's real name was John Ronald Reuel Tolkien. He was born in 1892 in Orange Free State Province, which was a former province in South Africa. (This makes being born in West Monroe seem not so crazy.) After his father died, Tolkien was raised in England near his mother's family. His books are mostly fiction about fantasy worlds, but they can teach us a lot about real life.

In *The Hobbit*, Gandalf tells Bilbo Baggins at the beginning of his famous adventure: "I am looking for someone to share in an adventure that I am arranging, and it's very difficult to find anyone."[3]

So many have read this tale and The Lord of the Rings books, especially after the blockbuster Peter Jackson movies.

The Hobbit is the first book in the series, and it tells the story of a safe, careful hobbit who simply wants to stay at home and avoid the world "out there." At one point Bilbo warned his nephew Frodo: "'It's a dangerous business, Frodo, going out of your door,' he used to say. 'You step into the Road, and if you don't keep your feet, there is no telling where you might be swept off to.'"[4]

In *The Hobbit*, this is exactly what happens to Bilbo. He seizes the moment and travels with thirteen dwarves in search of the evil dragon, Smaug, and stolen treasure. Bilbo encounters trolls, hideous monsters called orcs, mysterious caves, a strange creature named Gollum, and an even stranger ring. There are battles and deaths, and (spoiler alert) the great dragon is defeated. Bilbo becomes the hero he never imagined himself to be *all because he said yes to action*.

But Gandalf knows it from the start. "There is a lot more in [Bilbo] than you guess, and a deal more than he has any idea of himself."[5]

I think this can apply to all of us. Stories such as *The Hobbit* illustrate that any of us can be the hero of our journey. And, as Gandalf tells Bilbo in the movie, that "the world is not in your books and maps. It's out there." I hope *The Hobbit* will inspire you to grab on to the next big adventure that comes your way.

CHAPTER 3

WRITING

(MY STORY)

Nobody is more healthy, productive or
clear-headed than a person who has
planned and is living a meaningful life.

—DONALD MILLER

SO I READ THIS BOOK . . .

I think I could have started every chapter in this book with
those five words.

But in this case, a book truly changed the way I think about
my own life.

I knew of Donald Miller after reading his book *Blue Like
Jazz*. I had the opportunity to meet him when I met fellow author
Bob Goff for the first time in Canada (more on that later). Then I
read Donald's book *A Million Miles in a Thousand Years*.

It was like suddenly pressing the Reset button on my life.

Here's something I took away from that book:

If you watched a movie about a guy who wanted a Volvo and worked for years to get it, you wouldn't cry at the end when he drove off the lot, testing the windshield wipers. You wouldn't tell your friends you saw a beautiful movie or go home and put a record on to think about the story you'd seen. The truth is, you wouldn't remember that movie a week later, except you'd feel robbed and want your money back. Nobody cries at the end of a movie about a guy who wants a Volvo. . . . The truth is, if what we choose to do with our lives won't make a story meaningful, it won't make a life meaningful either.[1]

I had been thinking for a while about what it actually looks like to live a meaningful life. For me, the Volvo in Donald's book was an example of what having fame or a lot of money might be like. It's nice and all that, but neither adds a significant meaning to life.

Donald continued:

I think this is when most people give up on their stories. They come out of college wanting to change the world, wanting to get married, wanting to have kids and change the way people buy office supplies. But they get into the middle and discover it was harder than they thought. They can't see the distant shore anymore, and they wonder if their paddling is moving them forward. None of the trees behind them are getting smaller and none of the trees ahead are getting bigger. They take it out on their spouses, and they go looking for an *easier story.*[2]

Those two words at the end jerked me awake.

I didn't want an easier story. I wanted to write a story that had substance.

I wanted to be like Samwise Gamgee in The Lord of the Rings, talking to Frodo about the great stories and adventures they'd shared. I didn't want a simple and safe story. I wanted one worthy of sharing one day.

As I've mentioned, I had already started thinking about my future and trying to plan for it. I had started to visualize ten years ahead, to take steps to achieve the dreams I had for my life. But suddenly the ten-year question became: *What's my life gonna look like twenty or thirty years from now? Am I going to wake up when I'm forty and be disappointed with who I am?*

Instead of a fear or worry, it struck me more as a challenge. Donald Miller was in his mid-thirties when he wrote this book, when he looked back on his life and thought to himself, *I need to change some things.*

This motivated me to learn from his experience. Here was some sound advice that suddenly set a fire inside my soul. That's what I wanted every day to be about! Embracing the gift of life every single day. Waking up wondering, *What kind of story can I create today?*

Besides the story I would create, I also wanted to see how my story would fit into the greater story—the one written by God, the ultimate Author.

It's a Wonderful Si

One of the questions I get asked the most about our show is this: "Is Uncle Si *really* that crazy?"

I always laugh and then say that he's even crazier than the person you see on the show. The show actually dials him down.

The thing you might not know about Uncle Si is the life story he has created didn't start with our TV show. It started years ago when Uncle Si made the decision to love God. In his love for God, he lived a life worth acknowledging in this book. It's a life of faithfulness to his wife and family. It's a life of service to his country. It's a life showing strength of character. Uncle Si is someone you can always depend on. As long as I can remember, he's been at every family gathering we've ever had. Even if, as kids, we often tried to avoid him or watch him from afar.

If our TV show had never aired, you would have missed knowing Uncle Si, but that doesn't mean he wouldn't have made a difference. His life was still a life of service and honor.

It makes me think of what Clarence the angel tells George Bailey in the Christmas movie classic *It's a Wonderful Life*: "Strange, isn't it? Each man's life touches so many other lives. When he isn't around he leaves an awful hole, doesn't he?"[3]

In your own life, when you're not there, you leave a hole. Whatever you feel about yourself, someone would notice if you're gone. Most people don't know this about Uncle Si, but he never watches an episode of *Duck Dynasty*. If others didn't tell him, he wouldn't even know the impact his character has on TV. But Uncle Si's life is not about a TV show; it's about being with the people he loves. God calls us to be with people, even if we don't know why. Sometimes the "impact" is just being there.

A Plot Twist

Besides my big lifelong dreams, there were other things I wanted to change and strive for, other ways to write a better story in the moment. I started to look for ways to live for *today*, not just in the future.

I decided to start being more sensitive to others' needs. Fulfilling the needs of others is such an important part of loving the way Jesus did, and I felt like I was weak in that area. Remember, one of Mary Kate's observations of me was that I can be oblivious to the world. Sometimes when your nose is stuck in a book, noticing the world is a problem. Since I probably wasn't going to miraculously become more sensitive, I set a goal. I wanted to see major growth not in ten years, but by the end of the year. Then I worked my way back and figured out how to do that. The conclusion? I needed to do extravagant things for people.

I began by sitting back and observing the world around me. I know that sounds like a lazy man's call to action, but hear me out. We live in a fast-paced world where everything is instant and everybody is connected. But, ironically, everybody is looking down at their phones and living through social media. Basically, the world is passing us by while we're Snapchatting.

These days, deliberately choosing to observe the world around you is harder than you think.

Then I started to look for people who appeared to need things. Truly, in our super-connected world, we hardly know our actual neighbors, much less how to love them.

So I started with giving people car rides. Then that service grew to bringing lunch to people or giving candy to strangers. While I did this, I'd ask people how their day was going. I'd make a connection—a *real* flesh-and-blood connection. I didn't know what this would lead to. I was just having fun trying to figure out how to be more sensitive to others.

A couple of months ago, I was sitting in church and noticed a girl I hadn't seen for a while. I went over to her and sat down next to her.

"Hey, how are you doing?" I asked.

"Good," she said.

As we spoke, she showed me the bulletin that features everyone's birthdays.

"My birthday is this coming Thursday," she said.

I gave her a nod and asked what she was doing for it. She simply shrugged and admitted, "I don't really have any plans."

After that, I couldn't stop thinking about what she had said. *I should throw her a party.*

There wasn't much time to plan or invite people, but that didn't matter. It doesn't take a crowd to have a party.

Together with her boyfriend, we planned something great. It turned out that no one else had intended to throw her a party or had made plans for her birthday. But we got a cake and decorations and everything. When she showed up, she was completely surprised. She had no clue. The party was awesome. I hope she has a good story to tell about that night!

I didn't set out to start planning surprise birthday parties for people I barely knew. I just decided to start paying attention to what people might need.

Which led to doing the small things.

Which led, of course, to some pretty cool things—and some cool stories.

The Ingredients of All Great Stories

Let's go back and talk some more about Pixar. I like Pixar a lot.

Andrew Stanton, the writer and director of films like *Finding Nemo* and *WALL-E*, gave a TED Talk where he shared his clues to a great story:

1. Know your ending. Everything in a story is leading to one destination.
2. Make your audience care. That's the number-one rule. Every other rule needs to help with this.
3. Promise the audience that the story is worth their time.
4. Have your audience work for themselves and try to figure things out. Just make sure they don't *know* they're having to work for it.
5. Have a theme, and have things built around this theme.
6. Create a sense of wonder in your story. This is the secret ingredient to the best stories.
7. Tell the story in the best way *you* can tell it. Use your strengths. Use what you know. "Acknowledge what drives you," Andrew said. "Then, take the wheel and steer it."[4]

So how can you apply these elements of a great story to *your* life? To the story that Donald Miller was talking about? To the life story you are writing?

We've talked about looking ahead to the future and doing things to get to the destination. But how are those things part of a great story? Will people care about the things you're doing, the ways you're investing your time? Would it be worth others' time if you talked about it? Do you have a theme? Does your life have any sort of wonder about it?

Mary Kate's family is adopting a little boy. He's almost two now, and it's so fun to see the world through his eyes. Little kids seem to be amazed by everything because everything is new to them. They look for wonder. You can do that too. You might have to make a deliberate effort, like I did, but you can do it. You don't have to climb Mount Everest to find wonder. You can find it in your backyard as you're having fun with your family. Find it as you thank God for the amazing world around you. Seek to continually have your mind blown. There's something worth wondering about in every day.

Start treating yourself like the main character in your story— in the movie of your life. Be the fish looking for your lost son, or the robot embarking on a space adventure, or a toy in search of its owner. Or just be a teenager living in a small town wondering what's going to happen tomorrow.

A lot can happen if we choose to make things happen *and* find ways to make life more magical.

Today and Tomorrow

In 2005 Steve Jobs gave the commencement speech at Stanford University. I haven't stopped thinking about what he said that day:

> I have looked in the mirror every morning and asked myself, "If today were the last day of my life, would I want to do what I

am about to do today?" and whenever the answer is "No" for too many days in a row, I know I need to change something.[5]

I think most people would agree with that idea—I know I do (of course, you've got to factor in school, which not all of us are too crazy about to begin with). While it's helpful to approach each day the way Steve Jobs did, I think it's even better to approach life the way Jesus encouraged:

> But seek first his kingdom and his righteousness, and all these things will be given to you as well. Therefore do not worry about tomorrow, for tomorrow will worry about itself. Each day has enough trouble of its own. (Matthew 6:33–34 NIV)

"All these things will be given to you."
What sort of things? Only God knows that answer. But our job is to go out there and seek God's will for our lives, to begin living a great story. Don't sit around waiting to hear a clear message from God about His will for your life, or worry that you're not doing it all right. In the Bible, God clearly tells us what we should do, starting with these verses in Matthew. In other Bible verses, God shows us what doing His will means: feed the poor; visit the sick; take care of our brothers and sisters in Christ; love our neighbors; and love our enemies. If you're doing those things, you're on the right path.

In his book *East of Eden*, author John Steinbeck says, "Now that you don't have to be perfect, you can be good."[6] That's so true. God never expects perfection; He just expects you to try.

THINK ABOUT IT

1. In your journal, write down a narrative of the "story" you lived today. Go back and see if there are practical ways you could have made your story more exciting or meaningful. How can you do these things tomorrow?

2. What's the difference between choosing an easy story and a hard story? How does choosing hard things make us better people?

3. You can begin to change your story by looking around and noticing others' needs. Take a day and observe your environment. What are three needs you can fill for other people?

4. Now strategize about ways you can meet those needs— you can start small! Write down three small strategies (and do them!).

5. Look back to "The Ingredients of All Great Stories" section and answer these questions in your journal:

   - Does your life have a theme? What is it?
   - How is your story building around this theme? How can you continue to build on it in the future?
   - What's one "wonder" you've found today?
   - How can you tell your story differently than others? What makes your perspective unique?
   - What drives you?

6. Try this exercise: every day for a week, write down three things that cause wonder in your life. You'll be surprised by how addicting this can be!

Book Highlight #3:

A Million Miles in a Thousand Years by Donald Miller

Without A Million Miles in a Thousand Years, *I would still be working for the Volvo and the white picket fence.*

I'll refer you now back to my textbook on living a great story: *A Million Miles in a Thousand Years*. There's so much good stuff in here that it's hard to choose what to share (so you'll just have to go read it yourself). But one of its most life-changing ideas is this: "A story is based on what people think is important, so when we live a story, we are telling people around us what we think is important."[7]

Donald Miller thought he'd been living an okay story. But all that changed when he began working with a couple of film-makers to turn his bestselling book *Blue Like Jazz* into a movie. When he began working on a screenplay to turn his life experiences into a movie, he realized his life had stalled.

So Don set out on a journey to discover the world around him and ultimately find himself.

This book helped me view my life in a completely different way: through the light of adventure and promise. I've learned how important it is to write a good story for yourself, and why we have to let go of things that shackle our progress, like fear of failure. In the book, Don says, "The great stories go to those who don't give in to fear. . . . Fear isn't only a guide to keep us safe; it's also a manipulative emotion that can trick us into living a boring life."[8]

Don isn't the only one who wants us to live a better story; God wants that as well. We are the characters He created. We have minds of our own; we do what we want to do; we go where we want to go. While we're meant for exciting lives of exploration, God ultimately wants us to be characters who are transforming to become more like Him.

CHAPTER FOUR

CONNECTING

(WITH FRIENDS)

If you're going to play together as a team,
you've got to care for one another. You've
got to love each other. . . . [It's] the difference
between mediocrity and greatness.

—VINCE LOMBARDI

SO I FOUND A FRIEND . . .

One of my favorite passages is found in Ecclesiastes 4:9–10: "Two are better than one, because they have a good return for their labor: If either of them falls down, one can help the other up. But pity anyone who falls and has no one to help them up" (NIV). I've already mentioned my good friend Taylor Mayfield, but I've had many good friends. When I began my junior year of high school, one of 2-Mama's friends had a nephew who was going to start school that year. 2-Mama texted me his name and begged me to be his friend. That's not the best text to get on the first day of school. Nobody wants to be *forced* to make a friend, right? Friendships have to happen naturally. Well, the minute I met Peyton, I knew we were destined to be friends. He's funny, full of life, and loves God. Boy, was I happy that worked out.

My grandmother also got me to make another friend. Josh was from Australia, and he was in the States on a "gap" year between high school and college. He came to live at 2-Mama's house and spend a few months working at our Christian school. He's older than Peyton and me, so when I first met him, I didn't know he would end up being one of my best friends. But it didn't take long for the three of us to connect. Even though Josh is back in Australia and Peyton and I are headed to different colleges, I know we'll always be friends.

Josh was only around for a few months, but those months will go down in history as some of my most fun memories. According to 2-Mama, they were months of great danger, but I can only remember one crazy incident . . . which involved fireworks and an ice chest (you can probably still find that one on YouTube). I have much "safer" memories too—ones that have lots of late-night talks around the fire, laughing, a few movies, and (always) eating.

I hope you have some great friends in your life. Friends who have your best interests in mind. Friends who can help you get to heaven. Friends who listen to your dreams and are honest with you.

Friends are the glue that holds our lives together through tough times. If you've never read about David and Jonathan's friendship, turn to 1 Samuel 18 and go read it. It shows what a true friendship is like. Both of these men were strong and had opportunities to advance their circumstances: Jonathan was a prince, and David had been anointed the next king of Israel. Their friendship could have easily ended in rivalry, jealously, or a desire for more power, but it didn't. Their friendship grew through a mutual love and respect for each other. They had a connection that I hope you're able to find.

Three Key Ingredients

Throughout my life, and especially this past year, I've had the privilege of meeting a lot of "successful" people. I know the word *successful* is relative, but I'm talking about people who are doing extraordinary things. They're people I'd call "world-changers"— pastors, leaders, and authors who are helping thousands of people while living extraordinary lives themselves. But you know what? Even though they're "successful," these world-changers are still people; they're not any different from anybody else. God is just using them in some incredible ways for His glory, and they acknowledge that and let Him. (I'll tell their stories more as we go along.)

But I've discovered three things about these people.

First, when I've walked into their homes or offices, I've noticed these world-changers are surrounded by books. They read books. They write books. A big part of their world involves books because these people are always looking for wisdom (sound familiar?).

Another thing I've learned about these people is that they all had a dream (okay, I *know* you've heard this before).

And, finally, they surround themselves with great people.

When I was fifteen years old, I read *Good to Great in God's*

Eyes by Chip Ingram. In this book, Chip describes practices that all great Christians have in common. And guess what? Chip said these great Christians all read great books. You know what else they do? Pursue great people.

Wow—the same advice keeps showing up. That's when you know you need to pay attention.

A big and necessary step toward your dreams—toward writing your story—is to make sure you have the right people around you. And that doesn't have to start when you're out of college and working in your first professional job. It can start right now. I say it has to start *right now*, like with the friends you are hanging around with. Those are people who are sharing your dreams *right now*. And remember: always be open to new friendships. If I hadn't taken 2-Mama's text seriously or walked next door to meet a young man from Australia, two of my best friends would have never existed. Keep your eyes and ears open to where God is leading you—He may be building your friendship team.

Two Great Friends

Papaw Phil's story is pretty well known by now, but it never gets old, and I love sharing it. In his late twenties, after getting married to Mamaw Kay and having four children, Papaw Phil's life began to fall apart. He found himself lost in bad habits such as drinking too much and getting into bar fights. He actually owned a bar right before hitting rock bottom and finding God.

Papaw Phil was twenty-eight years old when he started over with a new life in Christ. What a change that was for our entire family, and what a legacy his decision left for all of us.

After Papaw Phil's conversion, he got very serious about

teaching others what he knew about Jesus. Nearly every night for many years, Papaw Phil and Mamaw Kay would welcome people into their home, and Papaw Phil would preach the gospel while Mamaw Kay cooked. After they ate and studied the Bible, Phil would baptize their guests in the river—right where he baptized me.

One Sunday morning after church, a man named Mac went up to Papaw Phil.

"I want to learn how to do that," Mac told Phil. "So can you let me know the next time you go out to share the gospel?"

Papaw Phil gave him a nod and told Mac he'd see him later. But then a couple of weeks passed, and Papaw Phil forgot about him. Until he received a phone call.

"I thought you were going to let me know the next time you went out to tell people about Jesus."

"Mac, is this you?" Phil asked.

"Yeah, it's me. Are you ashamed or something to call me your brother? I thought this following Jesus thing is like some kind of family deal, you know?"

"Hey, I'll call you the next time, all right?"

Papaw Phil hung up and then expressed his surprise to Mamaw Kay.

"I didn't think Mac was serious," Papaw Phil said. "Reckon the guy must be."

So from then on, every time Papaw Phil had a Bible study or went to witness to someone, Mac would come along with him. Sometimes it would be two or three times a week. This lasted for three years.

Papaw Phil and Mac just seemed to connect. They had more things in common than they first realized. Besides Mac also being an avid hunter, Papaw Phil and Mamaw Kay learned that Mac and his wife, Mary, had a story that mirrored their own: both couples had stories of brokenness that turned into redemption.

During their senior year of high school, Mac and Mary dated, and during their relationship Mary became pregnant. They decided they were too young and unfit to take care of the child, so the summer after graduation Mary had the baby in secret and gave her baby boy up for adoption.

For years Mac and Mary were haunted by guilt and shame. They eventually married and had two girls, but they both found themselves hiding things from each other. For Mary, it was the continuing guilt of having given up her firstborn child. For Mac, it was an addiction to meth that was ruining all of their lives.

Fortunately, God intervened. He led Mac and Mary to go before the congregation of White's Ferry Road Church, and they confessed their past and present decisions and expressed their need for help. They've written their whole story in a book titled *Never Let Go.* (Sorry, but there's another book title to add to your list.)

As I've said before, God is a God of surprises, so here's the rest of that story. Mac went on to be one of the original duckmen featured in *Duck Dynasty*'s first DVD series. But even better than that, Mac and Mary are now national leaders in the Celebrate Recovery program, which helps thousands of men and women suffering from addiction find hope and healing.

Here's one more weird connection Papaw Phil and Mac have: Mac and Mary are my great-aunt and great-uncle on my mom's side. Mary is the sister of John Howard, my 2-Papa, and the daughter of Alton Howard. I know it's complicated, but isn't it great how God moves? When Mac went to Papaw Phil for help many years ago, he never dreamed his great-nephew would write a story about it in a book.

God took two men with troubled pasts and connected them in such a way that they challenged and sharpened each other to become strong Christian leaders.

So how do you apply this story to your life? Think about what Mac did when he decided it was time for him to grow: he pursued a friendship with someone who was further along in his walk with God than he was.

No matter who you are or where you've been, look for people to help get where you want to go. Make connections that really matter.

The Making of a Great Team

I've always known that Mary Kate and I make a great team. And it has nothing to do with the fact that I think she's beautiful and fun to be with. Both of us understand and know each other. We both want the same things in life.

Here's a list of why we're a great team:

1. We encourage each other.
2. We don't keep secrets from each other.
3. We stay positive.
4. We don't try to force each other to be a certain way.
5. We accept our differences and learn to leverage them.
6. We don't compete with each other.

Teamwork means that you are working together for something bigger than both of you. You both want to be successful at whatever you're trying to do.

When you're part of a team, you have to remember that the other person is not the enemy. But you are battling an enemy who throws things into your lives on a daily basis. Fears, uncertainties, temptations, anger, pride . . . letting those things into a relationship chips the bonds away. The book of Ephesians says, "For our struggle is not against flesh and blood, but against the rulers, against the authorities, against the powers of this dark world and against the spiritual forces of evil in the heavenly realms" (Ephesians 6:12 NIV). That's huge. Any squabbling we might do as a team detracts attention from the real battle—and the real dream.

No dream can be realized without cooperation. In any relationship—whether you're building a church, a marriage, or an orphanage in Africa—when your team is working for something bigger, and the central point in your lives is God, you're headed in the right direction.

Biblical Connection

Another story of a great friendship in the Bible is the one of Joshua and Caleb. They were among the twelve Israelite spies chosen to check out the promised land that Moses had told them about. While ten of the spies came back scared and convinced they couldn't conquer the people who occupied the land, Joshua and Caleb had a different idea: "But Caleb tried to quiet the people as they stood before Moses. 'Let's go at once to take the land,' he said. 'We can certainly conquer it!'" (Numbers 13:30).

What confidence these guys had! While the rest of the Israelites shook their heads and wondered what they were doing in the middle of nowhere, Joshua and Caleb stood strong. They told the people not to be afraid, to remember that the Lord was with them.

And God rewarded Joshua and Caleb for their faithfulness:

"Of all those I rescued from Egypt, no one who is twenty years old or older will ever see the land I swore to give to Abraham, Isaac, and Jacob, for they have not obeyed me wholeheartedly. The only exceptions are Caleb son of Jephunneh the Kenizzite and Joshua son of Nun, for they have wholeheartedly followed the LORD." (Numbers 32:11–12)

I don't think it's any surprise that there were two of them standing at the end. Joshua and Caleb had each other's backs, and they were stronger for it. Despite all the anger and fear of the disbelievers around them, these two remained solid.

We're not meant to be alone in this world. Look at Jesus. He specifically chose twelve men to be his disciples in ministry. He told them to follow Him, and He'd make them fishers of men. Why did He have disciples? Why did He choose to work in a team? I think Jesus tells us why in John 14:12: "I tell you the truth, anyone who believes in me will do the same works I have done, and even greater works, because I am going to be with the Father."

The disciples were given a pretty big task: to carry on after Jesus went to heaven and spread the gospel to all the corners of the earth. Jesus knew that wasn't going to be easy, so He gave them each other, so they could strengthen and support one another.

Jesus gives us the power to do great things too, but He also gives us the opportunity to do them with others. Seek out people who will help you do those extraordinary things.

Start Today

In some ways, my adventures in discovering and growing and *doing* really started when I began seeking out others. Inviting other people in—whether as teammates, mentors, supporters, or even authors through their books—gives your vision the fuel it needs to help it grow. After all, you don't know everything, and you can't do everything by yourself! And thank goodness for that. Otherwise we'd miss out on some of the most fun and rewarding relationships life has to offer.

If you haven't invited others on your adventure already, why not choose today?

THINK ABOUT IT

1. Write down the names of three people you admire who would make good mentors, and contact them. Ask them if they would consider meeting up and giving you some advice.

2. Identify a few "successful" people who are good at what you want to be good at, and do some research on them. What books can you read by or about them? How can you find out what drives them?

3. Which peers can you trust to share your dream with? Which of your friends would you want to chase your dream with and why? (If you can't think of anyone, pray diligently that God would bring these people into your life.)

4. How can you ask these people for help in the coming weeks?

5. Look back at the list of what makes a good team on page 61. Have you seen any of these in action? How could practicing these things improve your friendships today?

Book Highlight #4:

Good to Great in God's Eyes by Chip Ingram

Without Good to Great in God's Eyes, *I would still be trying to do it alone.*

I want to tell you more about this fabulous book because it gives heavy-hitting advice and poses some seriously useful questions, like this one: "When you have run the race with perseverance and finally cross the finish line, what kind of assessment of your life do you envision the Lord giving you?"[1]

Chip Ingram asks this at the beginning of his book, then proceeds to give you a list of ways you can assess your life now and start running a better race.

This is one of those books I read and decided to apply to my life, and I feel much better prepared because of it. In the book Chip talks about the patterns he's observed in those who are extraordinary followers of Christ. Earlier in this chapter, I talked about Chip's advice to "pursue great people." The other nine assessments Chip explores in his book are ones I'm constantly going back to and striving for. Here's the list:

- Think great thoughts (like in your journal).
- Read great books (one of my favorites!).
- Pursue great people (your future mentors).
- Dream great dreams (like imagining your amazing future).
- Pray great prayers (and pray them at every step).
- Take great risks (and overcome your fears).
- Make great sacrifices (every one of them is worth it).
- Enjoy great moments (fill your life with joy and wonder).
- Empower great people (give back and focus on others).
- Develop great habits (because we are what we repeatedly do).

This book is a comprehensive, insightful look into action steps that will help you be the person you need to be. As Chip wrote, "God invites you to be a world-changing, kingdom-shaping follower of Christ."[2] This really fires me up, and I hope it will do the same for you.

PART 2

WHERE AM I GOING?

I'm not saying that I have this all together, that I have it made. But I am well on my way, reaching out for Christ, who has so wondrously reached out for me. Friends, don't get me wrong: By no means do I count myself an expert in all of this, but I've got my eye on the goal, where God is beckoning us onward—to Jesus. I'm off and running, and I'm not turning back.

—PHILIPPIANS 3:12-14 THE MESSAGE

CHAPTER 5

RESPONDING

(TO THE CALL)

Your assumptions are your windows on
the world. Scrub them off every once
in a while, or the light won't come in.

—ISAAC ASIMOV

SO I TWEETED . . .

A guy named Bob Goff wrote a book called *Love Does*, where
he, not surprisingly, talks about the ways that love shows
itself. And to give readers one example of what love does, Bob put
his phone number in the back of *Love Does,* so that people could
call him with any questions or comments about the book, or even
if they just wanted to say hey. Since love does crazy things like this,
our family decided to send him a message on Twitter (we thought
calling him might be a bit weird). Sure enough, he responded. Mom
e-mailed him and said she wanted to send him some of our books.

Bob, being Bob, responded with an invitation for our whole family to come to a retreat in Canada at the beginning of the summer.

Trust me: after you read *Love Does*, you will learn you have to say yes to mysterious adventures.

Each of our lives is full of calls to adventure—moments when we're presented with an opportunity to take a journey or go discover something. I think all of us can be heroes and heroines in our own unique way. But so many of us fail to accept that call to adventure. In fact, I think a lot of us are so busy and preoccupied that we actually miss the call even when it's right on our doorstep.

Our Call to Adventure

There are wonderful things in this world that I'd like to think I'll find in heaven. The sight of Mary Kate's smile. The smell of Mamaw Kay's chicken and dumplings. The sound of my family's laughter around the dinner table.

I'd like to think I might also feel the rush of landing in a seaplane, looking out my window to see Bob Goff standing at the edge of a dock. I can imagine stepping out and taking in the splendor of the Princess Louisa Inlet in British Columbia, Canada. My friend Bob will welcome me with open arms.

Wait! That *is* what happened. Bob Goff has pretty much created a homemade version of heaven on earth at his lodge in Canada. Let me tell you a little about how we came to visit him.

One day in spring 2014, my mother handed me a book called *Love Does* with colorful balloons on its cover.

"You have to read this," Mom said.

I love getting recommendations for good books. Whether it's seeing a post from someone online about what they're reading or a friend like Taylor telling me I *have* to check out a book, the best discoveries come by word of mouth. Especially if the person talking happens to be my mother.

Since I'd been reading a lot of nonfiction about God and faith, *Love Does* seemed right up my alley. *Love Does* is full of incredible stories about how the love Jesus talked about can be expressed in today's world. It describes love in action. And it's revolutionary.

Sounds pretty simple, right? As Bob Goff wrote, "Simply put: love does."[1]

My copy of *Love Does* has so many quotes underlined and circled and highlighted with exclamation points that it's barely readable. But here is one of my favorites: "I used to think God guided us by opening and closing doors, but now I know sometimes God wants us to kick some doors down."[2]

Now that's inspiring! When I picked up the book, I had been thinking about my dreams and my plans, but Bob's words stirred me and made my determination to pursue an amazing story even stronger. Here was a man putting his words into action.

I want to be like him.

What About Bob?

After reading *Love Does* and discovering more about the incredible author, I imagined Bob Goff to be this mythical sort of character. Like Santa Claus maybe, but I had read he's a lawyer so I had no idea what to expect when I met him. (There I go, putting people in a box.) I was already picturing the lawyer box Bob might fit in, but Bob is not someone who can be put in a box. He definitely lived up to my imaginings.

The short version of Bob's story goes like this: He had a successful law firm, but he wanted to start making a difference in the world. After the attacks on September 11, Bob spoke to his three young children about good and evil in this world. He posed a simple question to them: "If you had five minutes with a world leader, what would you ask?"

Challenging question, right?

Bob's children had brilliant answers.

Adam, who was seven at the time, said he would love to have the world leaders over to their house for a sleepover. Bob affirmed the answer and wrote it down on a piece of paper.

Richard, a few years older, said he would ask the leaders what they were hoping for, thinking that once he knew, he could start hoping for the very same thing. Another great answer, and Bob wrote it down.

Bob's firstborn, Lindsey, who was twelve at the time, said if the leaders couldn't come over to their house, why couldn't she and her brothers visit them? And better yet, what if they video-taped their meetings?

After Bob wrote down all these creative answers, he gave his kids the call to adventure.

"I had the kids put their ideas together in one letter. Then we downloaded the names of every president, prime minister, or dictator of every country in the world from the CIA website," Bob said.[3] Then he challenged his children to make it real.

His next step is where awesomeness comes in. The kids did exactly what they said they would do. They wrote to every one of these leaders, asking if they could come meet them. In all, they mailed hundreds of letters, and got back a fair amount of nos. The first yes they received was from the State House in Bulgaria, inviting them to the palace. It was the first of twenty-nine affirmations of "Absolutely!" It was also the start of an incredible adventure—actually, quite a few of them—for Bob Goff and his family.

Bob says in *Love Does* that he wants to "live in a new normal where I can reach out to people who are different from me and just be friends."[4]

So there we were—a normal family from West Monroe, Louisiana—accepting an invitation to go to Canada to be friends with this adventurous man and his family.

You Don't Need Specifics

We waited to receive further instructions about our trip, but Bob didn't get back to us. A week passed. Then another went by. Then just a few weeks before our trip, he sent us an e-mail.

"Hey, guys. Sorry I've been out of touch. I've been in Somalia."

I guess that's a good excuse. Some people don't respond to e-mails because they forget or become too busy tweeting and posting pictures on Instagram. But this guy—he was in Somalia.

"Here are the directions to our lodge—follow these to get there," Bob wrote. "Oh, and there'll be around 150 other people joining us."

For a moment we just looked at each other, wondering about all these other people. But there was never any hesitation about whether we would go. We knew that love doesn't question. Bob Goff had shown us that—that's why we were inspired by his book. There was no way we could turn down this adventure.

Even the directions were vague and mysterious. He told us when we reached Vancouver to ask for this woman and tell her we were going to visit Bob. He then said there'd be no phone or Internet service, so he would simply see us when we got there.

We live in a world where every detail and instruction is an instant search away on our smart phones. There's something refreshing about trekking into the unknown without having all the specifics. It's like the feeling you get when you ask for something for Christmas, and you know you're getting it. Your hope is real because you're confident of the outcome. You go to bed on Christmas Eve with a smile on your face because a surprise awaits you, but you already know what it is. We all had that feeling heading to Canada. Although we didn't know exactly what awaited us, we knew it would be great.

Making a Difference

We were standing in the first Starbucks that ever opened. On our layover in Seattle, we had enough time to visit the first of the now thousands of these coffee shops. I marveled at how it didn't look any different from any other Starbucks. It had the same wonderful smell. The same inviting feel that made you want to stick around. The coffee still tasted just as good as any other store.

Wondering exactly how many Starbucks are now in existence, I did what we all do—I Googled it. One statistic said there were 21,366 Starbucks stores around the world.[5] It started out as just one shop offering "some of the world's finest fresh-roasted whole bean coffees."[6] But a man named Howard Schultz had some big dreams for it. Big dreams—just like the kind Bob Goff and his family had when they started their adventures.

I've spent many days with Bob since our Canada trip, and he's told me about the time he visited Mumbai, India, in 2003. That trip took him on a harrowing adventure. He witnessed the horrific conditions that kids the same ages as his children were living in. The human rights violations were extreme and needed to be addressed.

Bob told me he knew one thing for sure: if you want to see how a country will prosper, see how they treat their kids. So he asked himself a simple question:

How can we make a difference?

Six words with a question mark. Sometimes that's all it takes. You start to make a difference by first asking yourself, *What can I do?* That is your response to the situation put in front of you.

This question Bob asked resulted in the formation of Love Does (originally called Restore International), an organization created to try and change a few lives for the better. Step one was an effort in India to free people in bonded labor or sex trafficking, or those who were otherwise exploited. In 2006, Love Does began working in Uganda, trying to better human rights and education. Right now the organization works in India, Uganda, Somalia, Iraq, and Nepal. The people who run these programs fight for freedom and human rights. They work to improve educational opportunities and try to be helpful to those in need of a voice and a friend.

How are they a voice for those who need one? They go into prisons to find kids who are accused of something but haven't had their case heard in court. These countries often have overwhelmed legal systems that can't handle all the cases, so the kids just sit there and wait. Love Does supplies lawyers and law students to these kids. The organization has also started to build schools; their school in Uganda is called Restore Leadership Academy, and has 330 students.[7]

When I was heading to Canada, I only knew about some of Bob's work. Little did I know that I'd visit one of these schools with him one day. But for the time being, we were simply wondering if we'd even manage to find his house.

There were five of us on this trip: Mom, Dad, Sadie, Mary Kate, and me. We all felt like we were going to Canada to live out some kind of dream. We had no idea what it would look like, but the first step was going through the door that had just opened. The key to opening the door of possibility was responding with a yes.

Just like Howard Schultz did once.

Just like Bob Goff does every day of his life.

This was the kind of adventure I want to keep living.

Marching Orders

Our seaplane floated over the blue water as it neared the mouth of the Princess Louisa Inlet. Steep mountains covered with dense forests surrounded us. Once we landed and opened the door to the plane, sure enough, Bob was standing there waiting for us.

"Welcome home," he said as he embraced us.

I admit, it was a bit odd to hear a stranger greet us in a far-away location with "welcome home." But it sounded like he'd known us his whole life.

And it was the best welcome I'd ever had.

He told us to put our bags in our rooms and come back outside. The rest of the people would be arriving shortly.

We didn't question Bob. You don't question him. You just go and do. Especially since he treats you like family.

We did as we were told and put our bags up. Then we rejoined him at the boat dock. Surely we were about to hear the plan. What was happening? What would happen the rest of the day? The rest of the weekend?

Nope.

Instead, Bob said, "Put on these band costumes."

Which, of course, made perfect sense, since we were in the middle of the Canadian wilderness.

Apparently the plan was to dress up in marching-band outfits and then ride on a smaller boat to circle the big ship, the *Malibu Princess*, which would be arriving with the rest of the guests. Bob told us that since we were the first people to arrive, we were now the "hosts." We would welcome the 150 guests as they walked off the *Malibu Princess*.

So we joined the counselors who had volunteered to help Bob for the weekend and made a long line to greet everybody. I'm not sure, but the counselors looked like they knew more than we did. It was an interesting sight. Some of the arriving strangers were beyond ecstatic, yelling and cheering as they greeted us. Others looked like they'd just been dropped into some kind of *Saturday Night Live* skit. I can only imagine what some of the people thought about seeing Willie Robertson and his family standing there saying hello and hugging them while wearing band uniforms.

As more and more strangers passed us by, I began to see faces that looked familiar.

I've seen him before. TV, maybe? The news?

Wait, is she a Christian singer?

I assumed all these people knew each other and also knew what they'd signed up for this week.

I never would have believed how incredibly diverse this group would be. I also had no idea how fun and playful our host would turn out to be.

Bob calls it whimsy.

Being Whimsical

The Internet has made everybody a critic. It has created a world where people take themselves *way* too seriously. That's why I love the segment on *Jimmy Kimmel Live!* called "Celebrities Read Mean Tweets." Okay, granted, most of the tweets that the celebrities end up reading need to be bleeped out at certain points. But what I love is that the celebrities aren't above poking fun at themselves while also showing how ridiculous (and outright vicious) our social networks can be.

Here are a couple of the clean ones:

"Ashton Kutcher needs to get hit by a bus. ASAP." (Read by Ashton Kutcher, completely straight-faced and serious.)

"If an alien landed here and demanded a famous person to eat, I'd drive straight to Adam Sandler's house with a net." (Read by, you guessed it, Adam Sandler.)

It's hilarious seeing the celebrities reading and reacting to these tweets, sometimes with humor and sometimes with no expression. They're having some fun at their own expense, but also exposing just how hateful the world can be when people feel hidden away behind their iPhones and computer screens, typing out words they'd never say to directly to someone's face. People think that somehow being anonymous excuses their bad behavior and the words they use.

Bob has a few things to say about words: "The words we

speak to each other should leave stretch marks, not bruises."[8] When those celebrities take mean tweets and turn them around, injecting a little humor, the words go from being bruising to stretching to something that makes us laugh. (Deal with that, mean tweeters!) The power of whimsy wins again.

Bob Goff is pretty much an expert on whimsy. In fact, it's one of the ways he discovers Jesus. It's not just about being silly or pulling pranks, even though Bob loves both of those things. He says whimsy is like smelling rain in the air. It's noticing the unlikely and unexplainable things that happen in your life and discovering evidence of Jesus. And when you're whimsical, you "leak" Jesus.[9] For Bob, doing things for others in order to get Jesus to love you isn't the point. The point is to allow Jesus to show up in mysterious and beautiful ways.

So Bob's goal is to create a good environment for Jesus to show up. And his tactic is whimsy. This is exactly what he did in Canada.

From the moment we arrived at his beautiful lodge in British Columbia, we saw this in action. Bob encouraged us to think outside the box, to be silly, to be ourselves. One of the things Bob does from the deck of his lodge is throw candy to people passing by in their canoes. He and his wife (who he calls "Sweet Maria") sent Mary Kate and me some slingshots and saltwater taffy when we first got married and went off to college. It was a great reminder to stay whimsical. As he says in his book, "Whimsy doesn't care if you are the driver or the passenger; all that matters is that you are on your way."[10]

I definitely identify with this idea. Growing up, all I've ever known is a family full of whimsy. Our family has always enjoyed having fun and playing with each other—pulling pranks and competing and simply messing around. One of our family's core beliefs is the importance of being able to laugh at yourself.

If you've ever been around my dad, you know that being playful, goofy, and loving is basically his way of life. He's passed that down to his kids, and I completely embrace it every chance I get.

I always loved having parties for my high school class just for the fun of it. I'm thankful my mom and 2-Mama have a lot of whimsy in them, too, because some of my ideas were a bit messy and required help. One time I threw a Jell-O party, where everybody had to bring two pans of green Jell-O to get in. When my classmates arrived they found big, blowup swimming pools in my backyard waiting to be filled with soft and slimy green Jell-O. We eventually filled them all up and proceeded to have wrestling matches in them. For a week, my skin color was lime green.

Another time I had a paint party where the people were the canvases. I told everybody to wear white clothes, and we filled the kind of squirt bottles you'd use for ketchup or mustard with a ton of washable paint. We had an epic paint war where nobody was spared.

Once, when we were draining a pond on our property because we were going to expand it, I had another brilliant idea. There was a giant hole of thick mud where the water had been. It was almost a foot deep.

It's party time.

First, I had to go find tarps. Lots of them. Then I got a water hose. I built a giant Slip'N Slide that went to the bottom of the pond. Then, as if that wasn't enough, I drove wooden posts in the middle of the sludge to set up a mud volleyball court. Needless to say, we all got dirty having the time of our lives sliding down into the muck and playing around in it for a couple of hours.

Even though the pond is full again, you can still see the volleyball poles sticking a foot out of the water. It's reminder of one of the many whimsical moments I had in high school with my classmates. The kind of moments that open life up to joy.

Unexpected Invitations

The four days in Canada turned out to have a kind of "unstructured structure." Bob and his team knew the schedule, but nobody else did.

On the first day, some of the guys were playing Frisbee golf. I didn't want to play because I didn't know anyone. But a guy named Ben wouldn't let me sit out. What I didn't know was everybody there was in the same boat I was in. As everybody began tossing around the Frisbee, I soon realized that none of these guys knew each other. And they realized the same thing. Eventually I just had to stop and ask all of them the obvious question:

"Does anyone have *any* idea what's going on?"

Nobody had a clue.

Everybody, however, had the same story. They had met Bob Goff or his good friend and fellow author, Donald Miller (yep—we just talked about him), in some kind of unique and unexpected place, then received the invitation to come to Canada. Bob and Donald planned this crazy event together.

The men and women surrounding me were musicians, songwriters, rappers, television stars, directors, producers, news anchors, bloggers, authors, artists, psychiatrists, doctors, lawyers, diplomats, Olympic athletes, chefs, Americans, Canadians, and Ugandans. They were from all walks of life. Everybody had received the invitation and directions. Not one bit of information about the event was given to the guests, but that was how it was supposed to be.

I met so many fascinating people with equally fascinating stories. Yet the cool thing was that nobody made a big deal about who they were—not even the famous ones.

If I hadn't responded to Ben's offer to play golf, I never would have gotten close to him. We got together and played every day, and I'd tell Ben who I'd met and he'd tell me the same thing. It was crazy.

I imagine heaven will be similar to this—a place where nobody is really sure what they're getting themselves into or who else will be there. Yet it won't matter. All the people have said yes and committed themselves to the whimsy, and that's what's important. They made a decision that seems like a wild leap. A decision to trust God.

In life, sometimes you have to make a blind decision in order to experience great things. You have to accept the call to adventure, which leads to discovering something great. When you consider accepting someone's invitation, don't look at who else is going to be there or ask about unnecessary details. Consider the person who invites you. Realize that saying yes might be the most loving thing you can do for that person, and it could be the opening to a grand new story. Have you noticed how we young people (actually, even older people do this) don't want to go on a trip or to a party until we know who will be there? That's when you need to step up and be the first to say, "Yes, I'll go." Our family went on this crazy adventure because my mom had read Bob's book. But my dad went because my mom said yes. And when you start saying yes, others will follow you on the journey.

This kind of yes is what starts you off toward the greatest story ever told—the kind that ends in heaven. The author of that story isn't Bob Goff. But Bob sure does love Him.

"Come and See"

In John 1:37–39, Jesus gave two of his disciples a call to adventure:

> When John's two disciples heard [John call Jesus "the Lamb of God"], they followed Jesus. Jesus looked around and saw them following. "What do you want?" he asked them. They replied, "Rabbi" (which means "Teacher"), "where are you staying?" "Come and see," he said. It was about four o'clock in the afternoon when they went with him to the place where he was staying, and they remained with him the rest of the day.

First, Jesus was asking them what they wanted out of life and what they needed.

These two men were given a chance to ask their Lord and Savior *any* question they could think of. And *this* is what they came up with? "Where are you staying?" But look how Jesus responded to them. Instead of telling them where he was staying, Jesus invited them to join him.

Love doesn't give just an address. It offers an *invitation*.

Those calls to adventure could ultimately be God saying to you, "Come and see." The journey might be long, it might be a bit scary, but it will also bring unexpected places and people and promises. You will surely see Jesus show up in the form of whimsy.

Maybe you've been invited on a trip that stirs your soul. Maybe it's a job offer, a scholarship, a program or event, a visible need, or just an invitation to hang out. Listen for the call. See if your heart moves. And if you hear it, respond, "Absolutely!"

Learning to Love

On our final night in Canada, Bob Goff's guests were treated to an amazing entertainment experience. A host of speakers and musicians led a time of singing and celebration. My new friend Ben was among them, performing as if he were among his family singing a few songs for them.

This diverse group had come together for one purpose: to show that love does great things.

Before this trip, I thought I knew some things about love. I'd seen it with my grandparents and my parents. Over and over again, I'd witnessed love firsthand.

But my time at Bob's cabin gave me an intensive, advanced, crash course in love. I wouldn't say I've mastered the *doing* part, but I at least understand the *knowing* part a bit more. It's taught me to ask, "What's the most loving thing I can do in this situation?" Then it taught me to respond—to take action.

Love is waiting and watching. It's letting others go ahead. It's letting them choose. It's this positive, breathless, constant belief in hope—an enduring hope that rises every day like the morning sun.

I suddenly felt like I wasn't a child anymore. I was learning to put away some notions and beliefs I'd carried with me for so long. I was learning that the world is imperfect and always will be. But God knows this and sees *me* clearly and perfectly.

No matter how smart or popular or adventurous or giving we might be, if we don't carry love in our hearts, we'll still be nothing. *Nothing.*

The Bible says a lot about love in 1 Corinthians 13, including the sequence about love being patient and kind and never failing. I had heard those verses my entire life. But in this wondrous, Narnia-esque land that Bob Goff had invited us into, I suddenly felt ready to put 1 Corinthians 13 in action: "Three things will last forever—faith, hope, and love—and the greatest of these is love" (v. 13).

As our seaplane took flight to get us back home, separating from the cold water beneath it, I tried to reflect on all the new things I'd learned. Before the trip, I thought I knew who I was and where I was headed. I really did. But then Bob came along and changed that. He demonstrated firsthand a beautiful passage from his own book: "It seems that what God does most of the time when He has something to say is this . . . He doesn't pass us messages, instead he passes us each other."[11]

Thank you, Bob, for telling me who I am when I didn't see it.

Thank you, God, for telling Bob who he was when he didn't see it.

Love goes on adventures. Love always will.

THINK ABOUT IT

1. When was the last time you accepted a call to adventure? How did you respond?
2. How do you recognize a call to adventure?
3. How can you create whimsical situations where Jesus might show up?
4. How can you explore the world besides physically traveling to new places?
5. Think about Bob Goff reaching out to world leaders just to be friends. What stops you from reaching out to others? Why didn't Bob let that stop him? How can you change?
6. Would you accept a vague or mysterious invitation? If not, why not?
7. What's the biggest question mark in your life?
8. What's the most memorable, whimsical thing that's happened to you? How did it affect you?
9. If you've answered Jesus' call to "come and see," how did you feel about leaping into the unknown? How do you feel about it now?

Book Highlight #5:

Love Does by Bob Goff

Without Love Does, *I would never throw candy at people.*

You might feel like you know everything there is to know about Bob Goff and *Love Does* after reading the last chapter.

But believe me—that's just the start. There's so much more. After you read the book, you'll feel like dropping everything and running out to do something extraordinary. You don't want to skip this book.

There are so many great takeaways in this book, but here's one that seems to sum up what *Love Does* is all about:

> Every day God invites us on the same kind of adventure. It's not a trip where He sends us a rigid itinerary, He simply invites us. God asks what it is He's made us to love, what it is that captures our attention, what feeds that deep indescribable need of our souls to experience the richness of the world He made. And then, leaning over us, He whispers, "Let's go do that together."[12]

Love Does is part memoir, part life lessons collection, and part motivational map for the soul. Bob shares some crazy, fun, moving experiences from his own life, and uses them to show us how to really be in relationship with others. We see that God is relational too—and there are so many opportunities waiting for us in the world. Not just in our family or our church or our comfortable job or our town, but out in the great unknown.

Bob's stories don't always have some grand point or illustrate some profound principle, but they do demonstrate the kind of love God wants us to "do."

Build relationships. Love. And go do things.

We can do this, Bob writes, and it's simple: "I think that navigating a relationship with a living God can be just that easy, and the math is easy too. It's Jesus plus nothing."[13]

CHAPTER 6

CURIOUS-ING

(STAYING CURIOUS)

Wisdom is not a product of schooling but
of the lifelong attempt to acquire it.

—ALBERT EINSTEIN

SO I WAS EXPLORING . . .

I think Mary Kate left off a significant trait that has always defined me. I'll give a few examples, and I think you'll get the point. When I was a kid I loved to explore. I drew a map of the woods surrounding my family's house, and my favorite activity was exploring—using my own map, of course—and searching for whatever I could find. I think my love of books stems from my curiosity about the world. As a kid I loved books about dinosaurs, snakes, planets, how people lived in other parts of the world . . . you name it, and I pretty much wanted to know about it.

As I grew older, this trait led to some pretty interesting adventures. One summer I decided to take my friends water skiing. Our family had gotten a new boat, and I couldn't wait to try it out. We hitched the boat up to my dad's beloved truck—he seriously loved this truck *a lot!*—and headed off for a fun day.

It couldn't have been better. I had three of my good friends with me (my mom later said she should have at least sent a girl with us to talk some sense into us), the weather was perfect, and the water was warm and perfect for skiing. We were on our way back to the dock, eager to get back home to a family get-together that included a steak dinner, when our plans changed instantly. I spotted a run-down old boat that was shipwrecked on the edge of the river. It was up against a tree, half in the water and half out. Obviously no one had driven this boat in a very long time. My friends and I inspected the boat and found some bullet holes in it, which made it all the more interesting. This boat clearly needed rescuing. We quickly decided to tie the abandoned, bullet-ridden treasure to the brand-new ski boat and drag it to shore. This was no small feat, but we did it. Then I called a friend to bring us another trailer for the old boat so we could take the new boat back home. The name of our new treasure (painted proudly on its side) was *The Happy Hooker*. Maybe the name should have raised a red flag. (The name is in reference to fishing, but it's still a little, well, *unusual*.)

With the new boat gone and another trailer delivered, we began using ski rope to tie the sixteen-foot *Happy Hooker* onto the fourteen-foot trailer. This should have been red flag number two. Keep in mind that the boat was curved and boat-shaped, while the trailer was flat. But ski rope had done the trick, and we felt like the boat was securely attached to the trailer; we knew that baby wasn't going anywhere. We made one call to tell our friends we were bringing a happy hooker home. And off we went.

Well, we almost made it home. We were seriously half a mile from our neighborhood when I, the driver, took a curve a little too quickly. I felt the shift and saw the boat in my passenger-side mirror, then I saw it in my rearview mirror, then I saw it in my driver's side mirror, then I saw it right next to me out the window. Then I saw green, then blue, then green, then blue . . . you get the idea. The boat rolled the trailer and then rolled the truck. Eyewitnesses said we rolled over four times, but all four of us climbed out the open windows with just a few scrapes, bumps, and bruises. Truly, it was a miracle that no one was seriously hurt. I wish I could say the same for my dad's favorite truck.

After a few phone calls, my family showed up—my mom started crying as soon as she saw the wreckage. It didn't look like the passengers in that vehicle could have possibly survived. Once we were declared okay, then the questioning began. "What is *The Happy Hooker*?" "Where did you get it?" "Why?"

After a few lighthearted jokes, the boat got hauled off, and we went home to heal and eat leftover steak.

I've learned that most of the time being curious and adventurous is a good thing, but sometimes it ends with your dad's truck at the wrecking yard and a lesson about never bringing home happy hookers.

Dancing in the Dark

Another thing that sparked my curiosity was learning to dance. I know you're thinking, *Why would this guy be curious about dancing?* Well, here's the backstory. The story you'll never read in any celebrity magazine and the truth about *Dancing with the Stars.*

I wanted to do it first.

2-Mama had watched the previous eighteen seasons and often talked about how fun it would be if one of us got on the show. So here's something funny.

I got a crazy idea right around the time the cast of season nineteen of *Dancing with the Stars* was announced on *Good Morning America.* It was September 4, 2014, when everybody learned that Sadie (not me) would be teaming up with Mark Ballas to compete on the popular show.

Soon after Sadie (not me) began surprising the country with her amazing dance moves, I started taking dance lessons.

In secret.

I didn't tell anyone. Not a single soul. I didn't even tell Mary Kate until after we were engaged.

I took dance lessons for three months. I began my private lessons right when the show started on September 15, 2014, and ended them around the time of the show's finale, on November 25.

Sadie (not me) moved to Los Angeles in September for intensive practicing, and after she left I decided to call one of my friends who was taking a dance class. I asked for the name of her instructor and then called her up.

"Do *not* tell anyone," I said when we first spoke. She thought I was joking.

So every Tuesday I would slip away unnoticed and park in the back of the dance studio. I felt like an actor training for a role in secret. I'd practice ballroom dancing for an hour, sometimes twice a week. And during the entire time I took lessons, nobody knew.

I had legitimate reasons to start all this. It wasn't just because my sister was doing it and I wanted to join in the fun. And I didn't feel I had to compete with her for anything (we're not like that). I honestly wanted to learn how to dance. I wanted to know if I could do it.

And I'll admit, I had this thought at the back of my mind: *They might end up asking me to be on the show sometime . . .*

It's not like you try out for *Dancing with the Stars*. They contact you. The show's representatives talked to Sadie (not me) for three months before it began airing.

When she was chosen, the idea swirled in my head that you never know what might happen, so why not learn something new?

The three months Sadie (not me) was on the show was such a wild ride. I already knew how awesome Sadie is, but a lot of other people fell in love with her and with our family that season. The first cha-cha wowed everybody so much that judge Carrie Ann Inaba declared, "You don't know it yet, but you are a *star*!" It also prompted tears of joy from my dad.

The show wasn't just a marathon for Sadie; it took its toll on the rest of our family too. We'd fly out to Los Angeles every Friday or Saturday, spend the weekend there, go to *Dancing with the Stars* on Monday, fly back Tuesday morning or take the red-eye back that night and get home around ten o'clock Tuesday morning. We couldn't stay in LA the entire three months because we were filming *Duck Dynasty*—plus, one of us had an important dance class to attend back home in Louisiana.

I knew I had to keep my lessons a secret. With Sadie and the show being so popular, I realized that it would make headlines if someone ended up spotting me in that dance studio. In fact, if someone came to the studio, I would bolt off to hide in the back closet. Once I hid in the closet for twenty minutes, waiting for some people to leave the dance studio.

I thought my dad was becoming suspicious when he started asking where I was going every week. I just told him I was working out with a friend. I could hear his thoughts: *I'm not seeing a whole lot of muscle development happening here . . .*

The most difficult person to keep it a secret from was Mary Kate. We would normally text all day long, except when she was in class. This worked out great, since this was the exact same time I was taking dancing lessons. I wasn't going to lie to her, so the only way to avoid her asking me what I was doing was to practice between one and two in the afternoon every day. So that's what I did. Mary Kate never asked what I was doing during that hour.

Once, while we were in LA, the truth almost came out. Sadie showed us a dance move, and then everybody started to joke with me shouting, "Show us a dance move, John Luke!" expecting a good laugh, because families are like that.

Oh, I'll *show you guys.*

When I busted out a dance move, they were all a bit surprised. They thought they were going to see the most awkward dance move in the history of mankind, but they admitted I was actually pretty good. I enjoyed the moment and didn't tell them I'd been practicing for the last couple of months.

My mom eventually came to me, as she usually does, to give me some encouraging motivation.

"You know, John Luke, you're not the most coordinated person in the world. If you're gonna be on *Dancing with the Stars*, you need to start taking dance lessons."

A good mom is honest with her children.

All I could do was smile.

Then I confessed, and she simply stood there in total disbelief. "What do you mean?"

"Yeah, I've been taking dance lessons for the past three months."

Mom still didn't believe me. "You have not!"

"Seriously. I have."

When I told Mary Kate what I was doing, she had mixed emotions. A part of her was like, "Wow, that's awesome, John Luke!" And another part was like, "Why didn't you tell me?" I guess there are a lot worse things your fiancée can learn about you than discovering you've been taking dancing lessons in secrecy.

Evidently the producers still don't feel that my joining the show is a good fit (yet). But hey, I'll keep dancing. There's still always that chance America might discover the sweet moves of one John Luke Robertson!

Tent Revival

I once went through a phase where I decided to stop whenever I saw something of interest and go check it out. This decision led me to discovering an outhouse race (for real), an armadillo festival (only in Louisiana), and a tent revival. I discovered the tent revival on a boring drive back from a tennis match. A tent with a bunch of people in it out in the middle of nowhere? Of course, I had to stop. Sure enough, there was a sweat-soaked pastor talking about Jesus, a lady singing at the top of her lungs, and kids running around the yard. I thought maybe I had landed on the set of *O Brother, Where Art Thou?* Before I knew it, I found myself on the second row between a man tapping his head with a Bible and woman speaking in tongues. My curiosity was so piqued that I went back a second night. Sometimes once is not enough if the discovery is that good.

Discovering Something New

The stories in this chapter have taught me two important things about staying curious. For one thing, curiosity moves you to action. Even though rescuing the boat didn't work out the best for me, my dad said he couldn't get mad at me because I had done such a good job of tying the boat down. After flipping four times, the boat was still attached to the trailer. It's a good thing my family values effort and hard work.

And I didn't end up needing to take the dance lessons for *Dancing with the Stars* (yet), but those hours at the studio came in pretty handy with Mary Kate on the dance floor at our wedding reception. Totally worth it.

Lesson number two: curiosity moves you past what you think you know and into something *more*. I've been going to church my whole life and thought I knew what worshipping God looked like, but the tent revival on the side of the road taught me that even if our worship looks different, we're still all worshipping the same God. I guess I already knew that in my head, but the knowledge became real when I experienced it in that big, white tent.

A Tale of Three Men

A college dropout began performing comedy in clubs. It was tough going, but he kept at it and eventually landed a few spots on television and toured for some musical acts. His offbeat humor finally got noticed, and he landed a spot on the second season of *Saturday Night Live*, performing alongside John Belushi, Chevy Chase, Bill Murray, and Dan Aykroyd. *SNL* appearances led to movies, including an early box-office hit that grossed over a hundred million dollars. The comedian and actor became a beloved household name.

Then there was a philosophy major who believed he would one day become a professor. The concept of the *non sequitur* fascinated him, so he studied the concept of statements that come out of nowhere and don't make any sense. This led him to a writing career where he bent logic and reason and added a comic flair. He went on to be successful in writing for television shows and live variety acts, as well as screenplays, essays, plays, fiction and nonfiction, and children's books. He even published a book of his best tweets.

The third man learned to play a banjo on his own during his teenage years. He went to college as a theater major, occasionally using the banjo to perform for others. The banjo was just a hobby, but he continued it for years. Even while having a successful professional career, this man honed his banjo-playing skills so much that he collaborated with a bluegrass legend and, to this day, he releases albums, goes on tour, and receives bluegrass music awards. He's even won Grammys.

Passion and determination can obviously drive you to succeed. But here's the thing about these three men (if you haven't already figured it out): they are actually not three men but just one—the multi-talented Steve Martin.

I would also call him the multi-talented and multi-curious.

If you look at his career, you can see he has woven all his abilities into a lifetime of performing and making people laugh.

His study of philosophy inspired his humor. His banjo would become part of his act for years. His writing abilities have helped him in the television, film, and literary worlds.

But not everybody can be that talented, you might think.

That might be true. But everybody can be that *curious*. It's in the curiosity and questioning that we discover more about who we are. And we can work at something year after year, as Martin did with the banjo, to make a passion into a true gift worth giving others.

Steve Martin discovered he had an interest in a lot of different things at an early age, and he kept learning them even after he became a huge star. His successes only fueled his desire to keep learning and growing and building those talents. Who knows where you and I might end up if we take the same approach?

Always Remain Open

Each of the great men and women I have met has a common denominator: their desire to gain more knowledge about the world around them, especially if the world tells them they've already arrived. Feeling like you've arrived means you're stuck. I could write a whole chapter about the things I'd love to do one day, but here are five of them:

1. Get dunked into the ocean in a shark cage.
2. Learn to play the piano.
3. See the Northern Lights.
4. Sail a boat a long distance.
5. Hike the Appalachian Trail.

It turns out my dad had a list like this when he was my age. He dreamed of doing everything from becoming a professional golfer and bowler to being on the Scrabble game circuit and being a karaoke deejay (which, by the way, would have been *awesome*). The truth is, my father has always thought big. He was a dreamer and looked forward to doing something great when he grew up.

There was a point in my dad's life when his appearance was very different from the man you see now. When he first married my mom, he was young and beardless with short hair and preppy clothes. (You'd have to see the pictures to believe this.) As my mother says, Dad wanted to do his own thing and make his own way in life. When he was young and beardless, he didn't see himself working at Duck Commander.

Neither of my parents imagined that Dad would end up taking over Papaw Phil's business, much less that he would appear each week on a TV show with the rest of the duck hunting family. My dad showed me how important it is to always use my imagination, to continually shoot for the stars, and to never, *ever* stop learning every single day. When he was about ten years out of college, the time was right for him to join the company, so he did. And he's never looked back.

I got to see my dad's ready-to-learn attitude in action when we were in Canada. He soaked up the whole experience just like everybody else. One night, while a guy was sharing his story with the rest of us, I noticed my dad taking notes. He was listening carefully and jotting down the things he was hearing.

It's easy to think your parents are stuck in their ways, and I'll confess, I do too sometimes. So it was really inspiring to watch Dad get excited about discovering something he didn't know.

Something he wanted to change about himself. Some part of himself he wanted to grow.

If there's one thing I know now, it's that my dad never stops learning. He could probably kick back and go the rest of his life without learning anything new, yet he doesn't. He is constantly studying and honing new skills. He's always gaining more knowledge. That's what makes him a great man.

I plan to follow in his footsteps, continuing to learn long after I'm no longer young and beardless—or at least after I'm no longer young!

THINK ABOUT IT

1. Do you know anyone who's seriously curious and committed to learning new things? If so, how has that affected his or her life?
2. What are you interested in? Crack open your journal, and make a list of ten things you find cool or interesting that you'd like to learn more about. They can be as random, small, or big as you like.
3. Commit to learning something new every day for at least five days. Chart your progress in your journal.
4. How can learning new things bring more joy and opportunity to your life?
5. Name a time when your curiosity led you to learn something new.

Book Highlight #6

Outliers by Malcolm Gladwell

Without Outliers, *I never would have known the reason I'm not a professional hockey player.*

First of all, you may have never heard of the word *outlier*. It was new to me too. That word just means "something operating outside of the main group," like the one cow that hangs out by the barn when all the other cows are in the pasture. Malcolm Gladwell, the author of this book, just seems to see the world differently than others see it, and he tries to get us to look at things differently too.

Outliers attempts to find the answer to what makes some people successful and others not. Gladwell looks at the idea that successful people are products of either nature or nurture, and in the book he profiles some of the brightest and the best, the most talented and famous.

At one point, Gladwell discusses what makes a successful ice hockey player. He discovered that the greatest ice hockey stars are strong, are driven, and—according to Gladwell— were born in the first three months of the calendar year (I was born in October, so there you go), making them physically larger and more capable compared to their less mature peers.

Gladwell points out something in this book that really resonates with me: "Practice isn't the thing you do once you're good. It's the thing you do that makes you good."

This book will convince you that we all can be extraordinary in our own circumstances, and we should never stop looking for opportunities for greatness.

CHAPTER 7

REBELLING

(AGAINST THE NORM)

*I am not afraid of storms, for I am
learning how to sail my ship.*

—LOUISA MAY ALCOTT

SO I RAN . . .

Track and Field Day in elementary school is a big deal. It's
the one day a year when the star athletes between the
ages of eight and eleven get to show off their stuff. I've already
mentioned that I'm not the most athletic guy, but in elementary
school, I still had a chance.

For some reason, I felt that my third-grade year was going to
be my big year—I just needed a little help to get to the finish line
way ahead of my classmates. I came up with a surefire plan to run
the fastest race I had ever run: I would fill my socks with rocks.

That was it. That was my plan. Pretty cool, huh?

For those of you who thought I was going to say something like "get up every morning before school and practice," I'm sorry to disappoint you. That would have been way too normal for me. No, I had a plan that no one in the world had ever considered. It was nothing short of genius. I had convinced myself that if my socks were full of rocks, I would run superfast because running would be so painful that I would be in a hurry to get to the finish line to get the rocks out of my socks. Well, part of my plan was accurate—running was extremely painful. It seems my motivation was right on target, but my execution had a few problems. Perhaps a more conventional approach, like practice, would have been more beneficial.

Motivational Mistakes

This chapter is about rebelling. In my own elementary school-kid way, I rebelled against the conventional wisdom of how to win a race and attempted to cut a new path. And I quickly discovered that while rebelling against the norm isn't always a bad thing, it isn't always *good* either. My motivation was commendable, but my method was not.

What does that mean? Many people view a tattoo as an act of rebellion, and it could be, depending on the motivation for getting the tattoo. If the motivation behind the tattoo is positive, then that tattoo can be a good thing.

History is full of rebels who had a good cause. Many of them are even celebrated and mythologized. Think about Robin Hood and his Merry Men, who were said to steal from the rich to give to the poor. We all know stealing is wrong, but because his motivation was to feed the poor, Robin Hood has been given a place of honor. Songs, movies, and books have been written about this man who was basically a thief.

Then there's William Wallace. If you're going, "Wait, who?" then think Mel Gibson in the movie *Braveheart*. The guy with the blue face paint. "They may take our lives, but they'll never take our freeedoommm!" I usually yell this line in my best Scottish accent about once a month.

William Wallace came from an undistinguished family and gained notoriety when he rebelled against the English, who ruled over him and his fellow Scots. After Wallace killed William de Heselrig, the sheriff of Lanark, a rebellion between the Scots and the English broke out. Wallace would eventually be captured and executed, but he remains a martyr and hero to the Scottish people. On my grandparents' journey to England, they went to Scotland for a weekend visit and now proudly display the picture they took with a fake William Wallace. It seems they are found on many street corners in Scotland—young men with painted blue faces, eager to take pictures with American tourists. (Kind of like the Naked Cowboy in New York City, except I don't think the Naked Cowboy ever did anything significant.)

Not all rebels are fighters who yell things from the top of their lungs. Look at Mahatma Gandhi. He was a leader in India's movement to gain independence from Great Britain. His form of rebellion consisted of resistance through mass, nonviolent, civil disobedience. Gandhi fought injustice through peaceful means and helped change the world; his peaceful resistance encouraged other rebels and history-makers like Nelson Mandela and Martin Luther King Jr.

I can't leave out the women who made history by rebelling and standing up for what is right.

Refusing to switch seats on a bus might sound pretty tame compared to bloody battles or mass demonstrations, but Rosa Parks wasn't any ordinary passenger going home from work. She was an African American sitting in the section of seats in the back of the bus for "colored" folks, which was shamefully normal back in 1955. When the white section became full, the bus driver asked the people in the row Rosa Parks sat in to give up their seats. Three African Americans moved, but Rosa refused. The grand canyon of hate between the blacks and whites in our country was too much for her, and she stood her ground. Rosa was arrested, and many view this as the moment the civil rights movement in our country began. Rosa Parks is great example of someone standing up for what he or she believes in.

There's another woman in history I have to mention. She is one of the reasons millions of American women were allowed to vote for the very first time in 1920. Susan B. Anthony grew up in a Quaker family and was raised to be independent and outspoken. She used those character traits to move her in a good direction—to fight for women's rights. She firmly believed that women needed to vote so they could look out for women's rights in all areas. It's odd to think that something we take for granted, like women's rights, was once questioned as to whether or not society needed to recognize it. Susan B. Anthony was a leader in this movement, though she died before women were given the right to vote. Sometimes rebelling for a good cause doesn't bring results until farther down the road.

All of these people fought for what was legitimately *right*. They took a stand. They held their ground. And while you might think your life looks absolutely *nothing* like those belonging to these people, or any of the other great rebels throughout history, I would disagree.

All of us live in a great war that has been going on since humanity fell in the Garden of Eden. Our lives are a daily battle between good and evil. History shows us that there have always been things society accepts as the norm, but they aren't for the good of everyone—things like slavery and restrictions on the right to vote.

Taking a stand requires strength and courage. The wonderful thing is, we know we don't have to do it alone. The Bible encourages us: "For I can do everything through Christ, who gives me strength" (Philippians 4:13).

Christ also gives us the strength to rebel not only in spiritual ways but in many others as well. Creatively. Emotionally. Relationally.

What's Behind the Beards?

I guess I was born into a family of good rebels. The beards are the first thing people notice about the men in my family. Truth be told, my other grandfather, 2-Papa, was one of the first to have a beard. Yep, he's all clean-shaven now, but back in the seventies he went from lamb chop sideburns to a full beard and kept it for sixteen years. He says that at the time, it wasn't totally acceptable for men to have beards. It seems facial hair has been a source of rebellion for centuries. Anyway, 2-Papa was just coming out of college and into the workforce, so he had to be strategic with his beard. He waited a few months, letting his sideburns get thicker and thicker, until he was established in his job, and then he let the sideburns unite. I like that. He rebelled against the norm, but he was considerate along the way.

My family's image is centered on being rugged, tough hunters. My dad's playlist is full of old-school songs like "Born to Be Wild" and "Bad to the Bone." Of course, once you get to know any of my uncles, my dad, or Papaw Phil, you discover men who put God first and their family second. You see a family who loves one another and prays around the dinner table. You'll even see men who aren't afraid to cry (Google "YouTube *Dancing with the Stars* episode 1 season 19").

A few years ago, our family put out a Christmas album (who knew, right?). The album had some old Christmas favorites and some new music written just for us. One of the songs was titled "Hairy Christmas." I love the words in the chorus because it describes the men in my family perfectly: *Like Jesus and Santa Claus, we've got love behind these beards.*

Yep, that's my family. They might look tough and, in many ways, they are rebels against a norm. But they're also men who are sensitive to others, love each other, and love God.

Rebels with a Cause

Every man in my family will tell you the most important thing to show others is not the crazy beard or a string of ducks, but that you are not afraid to tell others about Jesus. That's the only true rebellion going on in our family. We are proud to show off our faith to the world. That is the number one rebellion our family is happy to be a part of. Many have watched our TV show and commented on how brave our family was to end the show with a prayer. In all honesty, it wasn't something we gave much thought to. We sat down to eat and did what we do every time we sit down to eat—we prayed. Little did we know what a firestorm that would cause! Many thought we were rebelling against the norm by showing that we pray. But it wasn't a rebellion; it was what we do. Sometimes, if what you do isn't what others do, it's considered rebellion—but it's really just not being afraid to live your life the way you want to live it and not letting others tell you that you can't do something. It's been amazing to read the e-mails from people all around world who have started praying because of our TV show.

Let me give you a little pre–Duck Commander history. People thought Papaw Phil was foolish for following some dream of building a business out of duck calls. He had a master's degree in English and a job teaching school. He was geared up to fit into what the world says is the established world of adulthood. But to the shock of many, he quit his job, bought a small cabin down on the mouth of the river, and decided to support his family through commercial fishing while he figured out how to get his duck call business off the ground. Times were tough for the whole family. They truly lived off the land for their survival, as there wasn't much money for groceries.

After creating his first batch of duck calls, Papaw Phil went door-to-door selling them. A sporting goods store in Monroe was the first to carry them. He got another store in Shreveport, Louisiana, to carry them and also got some good advice from the owner.

"Get some printing on your boxes," the man told Papaw Phil. "You have to have something on those plain white boxes."

The Duck Commander logo came shortly after that—the mallard drake staring down with its wings spread. Papaw Phil kept building and blowing duck calls, and the rest of the family cut and folded and stuffed boxes full of them. My dad and all his brothers helped in the fishing business and learned how to dip the duck calls in the polyurethane that seals them. Mamaw Kay handled the bookkeeping. Everyone pitched in.

Pretty soon, Papaw Phil drove throughout Arkansas, Louisiana, Mississippi, and Texas selling Duck Commander duck calls, visiting every store he could find that might have any possible interest in selling them. Through determination and some redneck charm, he managed to build the business year after year. Eventually the $8,000 he made the first year turned into $13,500, then $22,000, and then $35,000. Every year the business grew bigger. It was all the result of Papaw Phil's simple plan:

Robertson Business 101

Rule #1: Make the thing.

Rule #2: Put the thing in a box.

Rule #3: Find someone and get them to buy the thing.

Rule #4: Earn a buck from the thing.

Rule #5: Do it over again and again and again.

He got resistance, of course. There were already much bigger names in the duck hunting business. They didn't want to have anything to do with some Louisiana hunter and his ten-dollar duck calls. But Papaw Phil kept making them and selling them and refusing to give up.

In the late seventies, he noticed that Walmart stores were taking the place of the small stores he'd been selling to. He knew he needed to get his duck calls into these stores, so he simply visited one and asked how many they wanted.

He was told he had to go to Walmart headquarters, but he decided to try another Walmart store instead. Eventually one of the store managers agreed to take six of them to sell. He then showed this order to the next Walmart manager, who promptly took all the duck calls he had.

Papaw Phil eventually sold about $25,000 worth of duck calls to the Walmart stores he visited. This prompted a call from the buyer at Walmart, wondering how in the world Papaw Phil had managed to get Duck Commander duck calls in their stores without the buyer even knowing about it. This led to Walmart and Duck Commander forming a relationship that has resulted in many sales of many products (maybe even this book!).

It all came from hard work and a vision. It also came from Papaw Phil rebelling against a system that said you had to do things a certain way. That initial buyer at Walmart surely would have told Papaw Phil the *correct* way to get duck calls into their stores. But sometimes you just have to do it your own way.

Because Papaw Phil wasn't afraid to go against the way business was normally done, he was able to get the attention of those who were doing things the normal way. Those businessmen and women noticed the one duck who was flying in the opposite direction, so to speak.

From VHS to DVD to Primetime with Love

Duck Dynasty wasn't the first time the Robertsons stepped foot in front of the cameras. From the very beginning, Papaw Phil had the vision to make videos. Just as he believed he had the best duck call on the market, Papaw also believed the family could make duck hunting videos that other hunters would want to watch.

The first video Papaw Phil ever made had humble beginnings. He rented camera equipment and hired a science teacher from Ouachita Christian School to film it. The title was *Duckmen I: Duckmen of Louisiana*. It was released in 1988 and sold about a hundred copies.

That's a far cry from setting a record for having the most-watched nonfiction series telecast in cable TV history (11.8 million viewers tuned in). But you don't just wake up and have something like that happen. Papaw Phil thought outside the box—*way* outside the box—when he started to film the videos. In fact, there really wasn't much of a box there to begin with. But Papaw Phil saw it. And even though it took quite a few years to make the second video, *Duckmen 2: Point Blank* eventually came out. It was followed by eighteen more.

When my father began helping to grow Duck Commander, he found sponsorship for things like the hunting DVDs. Eventually my parents took a leap of faith and bought half of Duck Commander, with my dad operating as CEO. He made lots of bold decisions as well, even risky ones like starting a show on the Outdoor Channel called *Benelli Presents Duck Commander* in 2009. The die-hard fans of the *Duckmen* videos suddenly saw a different kind of show—more of a behind-the-scenes look at the company and its operations.

This led to a bigger opportunity: a production company in Los Angeles reached out to Duck Commander in 2010, pitching to take the show to the next level. Two years later, on March 21, 2012, the country discovered the Robertson family in the first episode of *Duck Dynasty,* called "Family Funny Business."

The success of the Robertson clan didn't happen overnight, or even after a year or two. It started because of one man's consistent passion and vision, and that success continues today because those passions and visions are still worth fighting for.

Discipling a Rebel

When you think about it, the disciples were part rebels. They definitely went against the grain when they followed Jesus. Like Papaw Phil, they had to go against the status quo and leave their lives behind to join Jesus.

The twelve disciples were quite a diverse group who had very little in common. Their professions ranged from fishermen to tax collectors. Some had tempers; others struggled with doubt. One was an outright liar who would betray Jesus. They constantly saw the work of Jesus, yet they also constantly failed.

Jesus chose these men because they were humble and teachable, which is the opposite of what we know a rebel to be. They were ordinary men who knew what it meant to be poor and afflicted. Yet once Christ was crucified and rose from the dead, these men's lives were forever changed. Eleven of them would go out into the world preaching and teaching about the resurrection of Jesus and the hope this gave to the world. They were given The Great Commission: "Therefore go and make disciples of all nations, baptizing them in the name of the Father and of the Son and of the Holy Spirit, and teaching them to obey everything I have commanded you. And surely I am with you always, to the very end of the age" (Matthew 28:19–20 NIV).

Each of the disciples might have had hopes and dreams for his life. Things like providing for his family. Making a good living. Starting a successful business. Enjoying grandchildren in the years to come. But then Jesus came and showed each of them what true hope looked like.

Sometimes being a rebel means doing what is right when everyone else is doing what is wrong. Sometimes being the opposite of a rebel is pretty rebellious. Twelve men, who went against everything society had told them, went out and changed the world by telling a dark world that there can be light. Twelve men went against the religious norm to spread the truth.

Good Rebel, Bad Rebel

At the beginning of this chapter, I talked about some rebels with a cause and told you that those are the good guys. So how do you know if what you're standing up for is a good thing? Here are a couple questions I ask myself:

What is my (your) motivation?

If your motivation is to get back at someone or to show people you're better than they are, then you might need to take a few steps back and punt (as they say in football). In other words, you need to reevaluate what you're about to do and come up with another plan.

For those under eighteen years old, let's talk about our parents. We have all asked our parents if we could do something (like get a tattoo), and they have told us no for a reason we think is dumb. If we sneak out and get a tattoo just because we think our parents and their reasoning are dumb, then we are rebelling in a self-destructive way. It's true, there is nothing wrong with a tattoo, but there is everything wrong with actions that directly go against a parent's wishes just for the sake of it.

For those over eighteen, the same thought applies to all authority: your boss, teachers, government officials, police—anyone in authority. As believers, we're called to be obedient. Again, if you're rebelling just for the sake of rebelling, then you're in the wrong. Can you think of anyone who is constantly rebelling for the sake of rebelling and is happy? I can't. Most of those I can think of are in jail. Everyone involved is miserable. Which brings us to question number two . . .

Is my (your) motivation selfish?

God is very clear on the subject of rebellion. He doesn't like it when it is selfish. We are young people in an age when rebellious behavior is often applauded—and it's not behavior like William Wallace trying to save a country. It's a young woman hanging from a wrecking ball or a young man posting photos of himself urinating in a public place. I'm just being real here.

To me, rebellion is openly resisting what others consider to be the authority in some area. We've already established that there are times to stand up against the norm, like if you are standing up for others. But from the first man and woman, God knew a rebellious heart would be a problem to humankind. It didn't take long for Adam and Eve to think God's words were not important, and they sought to do their own thing. We all know what the results of that decision were: Adam and Eve were forever banned from the Garden of Eden, and the history of humankind began a journey that included rebellion against God, then forgiveness, then rebellion against God, then forgiveness . . . you get the picture. God gave us amazing opportunities for our lives when He created us with a free will, but it's that same free will that gives people the chance for selfish rebellion.

Proverbs 17:11 puts it this way: "Evildoers foster rebellion against God; the messenger of death will be sent against them" (NIV).

So before you decide to use your free will to do something rebellious—or against the norm—ask yourself if your actions are selfish. If your plan is something like Rosa Parks's was and you're standing up for the freedom of an oppressed people, then you're probably doing a good thing. But if your act of rebellion includes spraying graffiti on the neighbor's fence because you don't like him, it's safe to say it won't honor God.

One More Thing

Many argue that it's good to exist without rebellion, but I would argue that while some rebellion isn't good and can lead to more destruction, a healthy rebellion against what the world calls "normal" can be a breath of fresh air. Here's what I mean: If the world says all teens are irresponsible and eye-rolling crazy kids, then show the world that you're not. Be responsible. Don't roll your eyes when your dad asks you to take out the trash. Clean your room. Rebel against what is considered being a normal teen. When you do that, you will be like a breath of fresh air to your family, school, and community.

Use the gift of your free will to rebel in the right way. Look for opportunities to "go against the norm" that will bring God glory and tell others that you're not afraid to stand up for what is right. I'm friends with many believers who are forging a new path on social media and promoting good works, when the norm on social media is to be negative. More and more, God-followers are taking a stand and showing all of us that being a Christian doesn't mean acting one way in one area. Many athletes, musicians, actors, politicians are vocal about their faith. You can do it too. And it's a lot easier than putting rocks in your socks. (Trust me. That was pretty bad.)

Here's a passage that might help you stand up or rebel for the right reasons. It's a little long and, again, probably one you know, but don't skip it.

> Finally, be strong in the Lord and in his mighty power. Put on the full armor of God, so that you can take your stand against the devil's schemes. For our struggle is not against flesh and blood, but against the rulers, against the authorities, against the powers of this dark world and against the spiritual forces of evil in the heavenly realms. Therefore put on the full armor of God, so that when the day of evil comes, you may be able to stand your ground, and after you have done everything, to stand. Stand firm then, with the belt of truth buckled around your waist, with the breastplate of righteousness in place, and with your feet fitted with the readiness that comes from the gospel of peace. In addition to all this, take up the shield of faith, with which you can extinguish all the flaming arrows of the evil one. Take the helmet of salvation and the sword of the Spirit, which is the word of God. (Ephesians 6:10–17 NIV)

THINK ABOUT IT

1. How do you define *rebellion*?
2. Whose rebellious style do you identify more with: William Wallace or Rosa Parks? Why?
3. Jesus chose men who were teachable to lead a rebellion against the established religious beliefs. How do you think that being teachable is important to going against the grain?
4. Think of a time when you were motivated to stand up for something when no one else would. How did you feel after you did it?
5. Find another Scripture to show how God will be on your side. (Tip: Google "God is on my side.")

Book Highlight #7

Do Hard Things by Alex and Brett Harris

Without Do Hard Things, *I would never wake up in single-digit hours.*

It's refreshing to read a book for teens *by* teenage writers. *Do Hard Things* is one of those books.

Twins Alex and Brett Harris wrote this book when they were just eighteen years old. They had a popular website called *TheRebelution.com*, where they encouraged young Christians to rebel against low expectations that the culture had of people their age. They want people to "do hard things" for the glory of God.

What exactly does that look like? How can you resist the culture that's out there?

The Harris brothers share lessons from the Bible, history, and today to help teenagers know how they can do things that challenge them. They also share funny stories from their lives, mixed with examples of real-life teens who are doing exactly what the Harris brothers are writing about.

This was one of those books that not only encouraged my Christian walk, but also prompted the idea for writing a book myself.

Alex and Brett Harris are now in their mid-twenties, but they still want to do hard things for the Lord. "We do hard things, not in order to be saved, but because we are saved," Brett recently said in an interview. "Our willingness to obey God even when it's hard magnifies the worth of Christ, because in our hard obedience we're communicating to the world that Jesus is more valuable than comfort, than ease, than staying safe."[1]

PART 3

WHAT AM I DOING?

And let us not grow weary of
doing good, for in due season we
will reap, if we do not give up.

—GALATIANS 6:9 ESV

CHAPTER 8

RISKING

(IT ALL)

What is the point of being alive if you don't
at least try to do something remarkable?

—JOHN GREEN

SO I TOOK A RISK . . .

have a confession to make: as a child I didn't like change. I
know, I know: change is a big part of taking risks. My mom
reminds me how I would get nervous if she rearranged the fur-
niture. I wanted things to always stay the same. I was very secure
when conditions didn't require a leap of faith. As much as I loved
my grandparents, when my parents announced we were moving
next door to them, I felt like my world had been turned upside
down. I liked my house and the woods around it. I liked that our
family was in the house we were in. To me, moving was a risk.

What will life be like in another house?

What will I do?

Who will I play with?

All good and serious questions for a kid. 2-Mama reminds me that once when she redecorated her bedroom, I was so upset that she had to use a slipcover on one of chairs instead of covering the cushion and tacking the fabric down. This was so I could still see the old fabric underneath. She says (and who knows if grandmas can remember everything accurately, right?) I would go into her room and lift the slipcover, and a feeling of peace would wash over me. Okay, I was a weird kid. What can I say?

Fortunately, another part of taking risks is being adventurous, and I was definitely adventurous. As I've already mentioned, I loved wandering in the woods around my house. I would climb trees and build forts any chance I got. Once I picked up a wounded bat and had to get rabies shots after it bit me. I rarely wore shoes and constantly had a cut somewhere on my feet or legs. I didn't just climb trees; I climbed *anything* that could be climbed. Mom said she found me on top of the refrigerator at two years old.

My life as an adventurer started young. I guess that explains my desire to take all my groomsmen skydiving for my bachelor party.

As I've gotten older, I've come to realize that taking risks is a big part of life. And risk almost always involves some kind of change, from the small things to the big things.

Risk in the Small Things

Every day we're faced with choices. Not all of them are life-or-death decisions. In fact, most of them are small and simple opportunities. Yet when these choices add up, they determine what your life will look like.

Once I took a small risk that snowballed into something much bigger. At the beginning of my senior year of high school, Mary Kate was attending her first year of college at Louisiana Tech. We weren't engaged yet, and she was only an hour away, but it was still a stressful time for both of us. We were already talking about going to Liberty University together the following year, but that felt so far away. With our busy schedules, we didn't get a chance to see each other as much as we would have liked.

While I was with my old friends and falling back into the normal routine of high school and hanging out with buddies, Mary Kate was making new friends and trying new things in college.

This would be a test for our relationship. Did our summer of love really matter? Would the things we experienced and the love that grew between us keep us together?

That's when both of us decided to be intentional about our relationship. We had to be. We were used to spending lots of time together over the summer and even traveling together. But with school starting, us dating, her meeting new people at college, and me starting my senior year, we began to feel the strain of change in our relationship.

It's not surprising that a guy at Louisiana Tech started to like Mary Kate. She was in one of his classes, and he was in a fraternity. Let's just call him Frat.

One day we were hanging out, and up popped a text from Frat.

"Hey, what size do you want?"

Uh, what?

So naturally I asked, "What's he talking about?"

Mary Kate explained that he was talking about the tank tops his fraternity made.

"He's going to give me one of his shirts," she said.

Frat is giving my girl one of his shirts? Uh-oh. Cue the jealousy.

"So, wait," I said. "Are you going to wear it? I mean—it's a tank top, so what are you going to do with it? It's a tank top for a *fraternity*."

Mary Kate just shrugged. "I don't know. It's just a free shirt."

"No, it's not *just* a free shirt," I told her. "Don't give me that." I was imagining them walking around campus together in matching shirts, all couple-ish and smiling. For some reason my heart was beating pretty fast.

But she acted like it was no big deal. "We're just friends," she casually told me.

Gulp.

There are many ominous movie lines that have three words in them.

"I'll be back," from *The Terminator*.

"Why so serious?" from *The Dark Knight*.

Even "Run, Forrest! Run!" from *Forrest Gump*.

This whole "We're just friends" thing didn't sound so *friendly* to me.

"No, that's not how this works," I told her. "It's totally symbolic. He likes you."

"He just wants to give me this shirt for free," Mary Kate replied.

"Nope. If a guy gives you something, he's gonna want something in return."

Especially because he's a guy.

Mary Kate disagreed with me and told me it was "no big deal."

Three-word alert! Again.

Eventually I decided it was in my best interest to calm down, and I decided not to give in to jealousy. Who wants a jealous boyfriend anyway? I didn't want to be that guy. When she would ask me, "Are you getting jealous?" I'd reply, "No, I'm not." I was fine. She even showed me a picture of the fraternity tank top he was making, just to show me what a "not-big deal" it was.

I was like, "Oh, that's . . . fine."

Heart pounding. Again . . .

What she couldn't see was that I was committing the shirt to memory.

That night when I went home, I made my own fraternity. I wrote out my initials—JLR—in Greek letters and put the design on a similar tank top. Then I ordered it from a website where you can print your own design. Then, as luck would have it, my shirt came in first. I gave her my shirt before Frat got a chance to give her the one he was making. *Boom.* Tank-top wars: won.

And I'll be honest. My tank top was so much better than his. (By the way, my entire family got to be in the fraternity, since the shirt company had a minimum order policy.)

When I gave Mary Kate the shirt, I asked her one favor. "I'll trade you," I said. "My tank top for his."

Mary Kate decided to choose mine. She never actually got the other tank top, so maybe I did all of that for nothing. But you get the point.

Relationships involve risks we can take every single day. Mary Kate had become so important to me that I didn't want to run the risk of her being swept away by some tank-top-bearing college guy. So I took a little risk myself—I had to do something to show her how I felt, even if it was kind of nuts.

But risk doesn't always have to be about doing something. With the tank-top experience, the risk I took wasn't making a shirt for Mary Kate; it was opening up and telling her how much I cared, even admitting that something insignificant like getting a shirt from a friend could make me jealous. Honesty and vulnerability are risky sometimes, but luckily for me, it paid off—and eventually she let me give her a ring to go with that tank top.

Risk in the Big Things

In December 2013, the equivalent of a tsunami hit the Robertson family. As Dad put it in an interview, "Oh, my father, he made Christmas very interesting for us."[1]

A reporter for a big magazine reached out to Papaw Phil to do an in-depth interview. This was nothing unusual, except for the fact that this isn't Papaw Phil's favorite thing to do. He agreed to do the interview and spent a considerable amount of time with a reporter sharing about duck hunting and life in Louisiana.

If you've ever met or heard my papaw, you know he speaks his mind and always shares from his heart. This is exactly what he did. He didn't pull any punches about his views—even the ones that aren't so popular these days.

When the interview was posted, the media had a field day. It became such a firestorm of discussion that he was temporarily suspended from the show.

It was a tough time for everybody in our family, especially Mamaw Kay. However, there wasn't any question what our family would do: we stood behind Papaw Phil and issued an official statement:

> While some of Phil's unfiltered comments to the reporter were coarse, his beliefs are grounded in the teachings of the Bible. . . . Phil is a Godly man who follows what the Bible says are the greatest commandments: "Love the Lord your God with all your heart" and "Love your neighbor as yourself." Phil would never incite or encourage hate.[2]

There was no question in our minds: the show couldn't go on without Papaw Phil being a part of it. The last part of the statement went like this: "We have had a successful working relationship with A&E but, as a family, we cannot imagine the show going forward without our patriarch at the helm. We are in discussion with A&E to see what that means for the future of *Duck Dynasty*."[3]

This was the risky part. Our TV show, which had become jobs for our family, was in danger of being pulled. That would affect many other people who had come to work for us. But it was the decision we felt we had to make, no matter the risk. Eight days after announcing his suspension, the network reinstated Papaw Phil.

My grandfather has been very open about his wild days and his own messy life. He knows what sin looks like and how it can destroy everything in its path. He's spent his life after coming to faith sharing the message of Jesus Christ. Yes, it's definitely in Phil Robertson's own unique way, but it's only because of where his heart is coming from.

My mom said this about Papaw Phil: "Anybody who knows

Phil . . . knows that he is about love, and his message is about God's love, God's grace and His forgiveness, ultimately."

Having faith and sharing it are certainly risky. When you're under attack, it's even riskier to take a stand. Especially when you're in the public eye and under intense scrutiny.

As my father says in the movie *God's Not Dead*, everything belongs to God, including our lives. All the other things—the fame and fortune and success—are temporary.

It sure makes a lot more sense to take a risk for God. There's nothing temporary about our eternal Father.

Another Risk Taker

Did you hear the one about the lawyer who quit his job to play with toys for a living?

Sounds like the start of a joke, but it's actually a true story. Nathan Sawaya was a corporate attorney practicing law at a firm in New York City. To relieve stress, he would build sculptures out of a variety of materials. One day, he got the idea to make a self-portrait out of LEGO blocks. After receiving tons of affirmation from friends and family, Nathan launched a website to show off his pieces.

In 2004, his site Brickartist.com crashed because of too much traffic. This was the day Nathan decided to leave his job and create LEGO sculptures *for a living*. His sculptures now sell for tens of thousands of dollars. He's gone on to produce multiple museum exhibits, and his work has even been featured during the Academy Awards.

It's one thing to have a passion and a talent for something. It's another to work hard doing that very thing.

And it's a *whole* other thing to take a leap of faith and risk everything to pursue that thing.

Whether it's in business, the creative arts, sports, or simply life, every truly successful person you encounter or learn about has taken that leap.

Liberty

"The world needs your leadership. You are in a position to give it because of where you are, what you know, what you believe in, and your belief in a God that is more powerful than any force on this earth."[4]

It was February 18, 2015. Sean Hannity, the television and radio host and best-selling author, was speaking at Liberty University at convocation. He challenged the students to be bold. He said:

> We need your wisdom; we need your brilliance; we need your power; we need your courage. You are all young people; I want you to be courageous in your life. Feel the fear and do it anyway. I want you to look from the high dive. I want you to leap; I want you to jump . . . even if you are scared. I want you to be the leadership that is going to save this country. If you do this, then I will tell you that there is no evil, there is no economy, that cannot be saved.[5]

I was excited to be there to hear these words. I was also excited to be up on the stage with him after I had just shared a story about my own journey toward jumping into something big.

A month earlier, in January, I had seen a news story about

a twenty-two-thousand-square-foot school building that some people were giving away for free. It wasn't far from where I live. It's in a small town of a few hundred people, three churches, and one massive old school building that was now just sitting there empty.

The previous owner was in his eighties when he bought the building and started renovating it. He put a few million dollars into the renovation before he passed away. The building wasn't finished, and it was still going to cost around a million dollars to complete. So it sat empty and untouched for almost a decade.

After hearing about this building, I once again thought of Bob Goff saying,

"If you want more faith, do more stuff."

This was what Bob had been telling me during our trip to Uganda. And he didn't just tell it; he showed it. I saw the fruits of his labor. I saw what *doing more stuff* actually looked like, and it looked pretty incredible. There were actual smiles attached to the work Bob had been doing.

I wanted more faith. So I called these people and asked if I could have the school. The people I originally spoke to told me yes, so we started the process of getting the paperwork done.

The owners of the building were, naturally, interested in what my plans were for the building, but as each day passed, it looked like things were falling into place.

Sure, I received some resistance. Starting with my father.

"You're buying a *what*?" Dad asked me in disbelief.

"A building that used to be a school. But I'm not buying it. They're giving it away."

"John Luke, nothing in this world is free."

"This building is free," I said.

"And how *big* is this building?"

"It's twenty-two thousand square feet."

He shook his head. "And it's just ready to go—just like that?"

"No," I replied. "It needs a little work."

"How much?"

"Well, a lot of work . . ."

Then I told Dad my plans, and he understood. Plus, he knew that once I'd gotten the idea in my head, it was going to be hard to stop!

The building had four owners, which meant it was going to take four signatures for me to get the property. I knew this was a potential problem, but this didn't discourage me. The papers were in process, just like the plans for renovations were, and I assumed everything would be good to go soon.

In February of my senior year of high school, I visited Liberty University with one of my friends. At a hockey game, I ran into the president of the university, Jerry Falwell Jr. I shared the story about buying this school, and Falwell was so excited by it that he told me I had to share this at convocation, which is a time when the whole school is together for singing, worship, and listening to speakers. So that's how I ended up on that stage with Sean Hannity. At that point, I thought the deal was all done and everything had gone through.

What better time to share the whole story than here in front of so many students? These people will be my classmates in another year.

I got on stage and shared the whole backstory about the building. Then I got to the "why." My goal was to turn the old school building into a recovery home for women getting out of prostitution. It was for victims of human trafficking who were finally starting their lives over.

I had partnered with someone in Louisiana doing amazing work with a ministry to rescue girls and women from sex trafficking. This building could be the piece of the puzzle missing from their ministry—a place where these girls and women could go for help and healing.

So, in front of fifteen thousand students, I publicly shared my dream for the first time. When it was all over, I walked off the stage before Sean Hannity was about to speak, but he grabbed me and said, "Hey, sit down for a second." This was right up there *on the stage*. So I sort of awkwardly grabbed a chair and stayed while Hannity began giving a speech about young people following their dreams and making America a better place.

Then he said something incredible.

"I'm going to give John Luke Robertson $50,000 to fund his building."

It was absolutely crazy. I began to cry while the audience all applauded and said a collective "*Wow*."

If you want more faith, do more stuff.

Thank You, God.

Deciding to take the free building and renovate it was a huge risk. But then again, it didn't feel like much of a risk at the time.

I would understand just how risky this was a few months later when everything fell apart. Literally.

But that's the next chapter.

Unlikely Heroes

Every follower of Christ is a risk taker. God asks us to follow Him and step out of our comfort zones. He equips the Holy Spirit to give us the courage and wisdom to do it. He also allows us to be surrounded by wise people who help show us the way.

I admire the men and women of the Old Testament who believed before Jesus ever came down to earth. They lived and breathed without the assistance of the Holy Spirit. They were true risk takers, to say the least.

Just look at one of the most obvious ones: David.

Who doesn't love the story of David and Goliath? David is a symbol of bravery—of something small battling something big. David, of course, was the young shepherd who spoke out against the giant while standing on the battle lines: "Who is this pagan Philistine anyway, that he is allowed to defy the armies of the living God?" David asked (1 Samuel 17:26).

David shouldn't have even been there in the first place. He wasn't a soldier; he was the youngest son in his family, and he spent most of his time in the hills with sheep. But it didn't matter. He stepped foot on the battleground with the Lord on his side, and the rest is history.

This is one of those Bible stories we hear so often that we almost treat it like a fairy tale, or a Disney movie. Of course, Disney movies don't end with the bad guy's head being cut off with a sword, but you know what I mean.

God told us this story, and countless others in the Bible, because He knew how difficult it would be to stand up to the enemy. It will always be difficult to stand up to fear, and to great challenges too. People might shut you down because you're young, just as they did with David. If you try to make a stand or take a risk, it's just going to happen. But that doesn't mean you shouldn't stand up, and it doesn't mean you aren't chosen by God to fulfill a purpose.

Age and Circumstances Don't Matter

It's easy to think about taking a leap of faith, standing strong, and speaking out loud for God when you're older. But God doesn't want us to wait. The Bible is full of young men and women God chose to be important witnesses. Besides David, I want to tell you about another great example of someone God called at an early age. But at first, this person resisted the call:

> "O Sovereign LORD," I said, "I can't speak for you! I'm too young!"
>
> The LORD replied, "Don't say, 'I'm too young,' for you must go wherever I send you and say whatever I tell you. And don't be afraid of the people, for I will be with you and will protect you. I, the LORD, have spoken!"

This is Jeremiah 1:6–8, where the great Old Testament prophet receives his calling. God would ask Jeremiah to undertake a mighty task: warning the kings of Judah about the coming judgment. And without going into all the historical details, let me point out that this was a pretty terrifying thing to ask of someone. Especially someone young. It wasn't like putting a tweet out about how bad of a job you feel the president might be doing. God was asking Jeremiah to put his life at risk, since the kings back then controlled *everything*.

It took quite a lot of strength to go to a king and say something like: "Yes, hello, King. God has appointed me as His messenger to tell you that your sins and the sins of all your nation's people are being judged by Him. Invaders from the north are coming to destroy Jerusalem for breaking their covenant with God. Oh, and I have a full list of all the bad things you guys have done. Can you sit down for a moment—oh, wait, you're already on your throne. Well, this isn't going to be pretty, but here goes . . ."

Jeremiah was persecuted for doing this. His life was one of hardship and misery. At different times he was put into stocks, arrested, beaten, ridiculed, and hated (Jeremiah 20), but God promised Jeremiah protection:

> "They will fight against you like an attacking army, but I will make you as secure as a fortified wall of bronze. They will not conquer you, for I am with you to protect and rescue you. I, the LORD, have spoken!" (15:20)

Many people might have viewed Jeremiah's life as a failure. He spent most of his life prophesying to a group of people who refused to listen and, instead, did him harm. Jeremiah's confessions in the Bible (better known as the book of Lamentations) show the prophet's inner turmoil. God called him to do an incredibly difficult job. He didn't promise that Jeremiah would find success; He only told Jeremiah that He would protect him.

God has plans for us, regardless of how young we might be or how difficult that task might get. The world needs strong men and women, like Jeremiah, to go out and do bold things. Risks are right up God's alley. He loves to protect those He sends to battle.

I love this verse found in 2 Corinthians 4:7–9:

> But we have this treasure in jars of clay to show that this all-surpassing power is from God and not from us. We are hard pressed on every side, but not crushed; perplexed, but not in

despair; persecuted, but not abandoned; struck down, but not destroyed. (NIV)

Anytime I feel hard pressed, in despair, persecuted, or abandoned, this verse reminds me that God's all-surpassing power is standing beside me, giving me strength and courage.

Ask for God's Guidance

Before taking a leap of faith, we need to make sure our plans line up with what God wants us to do. The Old Testament shares examples of God literally speaking to men and telling them exactly how they should take leaps of faith: men like Abraham, Moses, and Jeremiah.

Earlier I shared the story about my great-grandfather, Alton Howard, and how he started Howard Publishing because he loved hymns and wanted to create a hymnal. Eventually his son, John Howard, took over Howard Publishing, and it grew from a small, single-book publisher to one of the most respected Christian publishing companies in America.

When I was little, I would visit my grandparents at work. I would go up the stairs and straight for the snack room (probably the best place for a kid in an office). At the time, I didn't understand what Howard Publishing did and the impact it was making on the world. Now I get it, especially after writing this book. In fact, my grandparents have helped guide me and the rest of our family in our adventures in publishing.

After Howard Publishing grew to forty employees, a large office, and an even larger warehouse, a big New York publishing company came to them, wanting to buy Howard Publishing.

This was a hard decision. The company had been in the family for so long. Plus, 2-Papa loved his employees, and he knew that selling the company would mean that some people would lose their jobs. His father, Papaw Howard, was still alive at this time, but he was very sick. 2-Papa says this was a time when he really didn't know what to do.

2-Papa got the New York company's offer to buy Howard Publishing right before our annual family beach trip. Every time we go on a beach trip, we like to search for sand dollars. They're pretty thin and fragile, so finding a whole one is extremely rare. If one of us ever finds one, the whole family runs to look at it. That summer, after the New York publisher's offer, 2-Papa said he did something he rarely does—he prayed for God to send him a sign.

"God, if you think it's best for me to sell Howard, let me find a sand dollar," my grandpa prayed.

I know it sounds pretty crazy, but wait until you hear the rest of the story.

Later that week during the family trip, we were hunting for sand dollars. For the first and only time in our beach history, one of our family members stepped on *an entire bed* of sand dollars. There were thousands of them. We brought as many as we could to the back porch of our beach house, but we finally had to stop. There were too many. 2-Papa took that as a pretty clear message from God. He went back and accepted the offer to sell the company.

Imagine selling this company that your father created and that you had helped grow into something special. It was quite a risk for him. But God spoke pretty clearly.

We also can see the fruits of this decision.

Howard Publishing was sold just as Duck Commander started growing. Several of the Howard Publishing employees went straight to work for Duck Commander. This, of course, was a great relief for my grandparents. As for the Howard Publishing warehouse? Well, this is the Duck Commander warehouse you see in the *Duck Dynasty* episodes. Now, instead of housing books, it houses duck calls and all our family's offices. And now 2-Papa works full-time at Duck Commander too.

My grandfather took a risk letting go of something that meant so much to him. God had a plan. He always does.

We just have to know that He does and trust Him with it.

Knowing God's Will

In my nineteen years of life (which I know isn't that long), I've come to realize there are not always going to be sand dollars that show up out of the blue. Sometimes you can find God's plans for you in other ways.

Go read.

My friend Peyton's grandpa used to say, "Stay in a place where God can bless you." And the easiest place God can bless you is through His own words that He gave to you. You know how Solomon said in Ecclesiastes that there's nothing new under the sun (1:9)? Well, he was right. Chances are that if you're facing a problem, somebody in the Bible faced something similar too. It might not be *exactly* similar (Instagram wouldn't be around for another couple thousand years), but people have generally remained the same since the dawn of time: they laugh, they cry, and they all love food. So if you've got a problem (you're jealous;

your friend stole your boyfriend; you're super worried about deciding your next step after high school), open your Bible and see how somebody else dealt with it.

Seek wisdom.

When I first got a sailboat, I was so eager to take it out on the water. But the day I wanted to take it out, the weather was horrible: the wind was blowing, and waves were super rough. I wanted to take it out *so* badly, and hey, even if it gets a little dicey, my boating activities have usually ended up pretty okay (remember *The Happy Hooker*?). But just to be safe, I asked my dad, who's a much more experienced sailor than I am, what I should do—and he said to wait for a better day. Dad knew that I was caught up in the moment, and just wanted to try out my new thing instead of actually thinking about the consequences of what I was doing. It could've been super dangerous. I'm glad I actually thought about asking the advice of someone much wiser than me. If you're stuck on a question, go ask someone whose opinion you trust. God gave you those people for a reason.

Keep praying.

Do you stumble over your own words sometimes? Ever have a bunch of thoughts rumbling around in your head, and you know you kind of feel a certain way, but if somebody asked you what you feel and why you feel that way, you just sort of . . . freeze? Praying can help you out with that.

Praying is awesome—you get to talk to God, and you get to do it in a way that you feel comfortable. In front of others? Okay. By yourself? God's good with that, too, especially if there's something you're wrestling with. Praying helps you focus your thoughts, and lay what's on your heart before a God who really cares about you. And the cool thing is that *you don't even have to know what to pray for*. In Romans 8, Paul wrote:

> The [Holy] Spirit helps us in our weakness. We do not know what we ought to pray for, but the Spirit himself intercedes for us through wordless groans. And . . . the Spirit intercedes for God's people in accordance with the will of God.
>
> And we know that in all things God works for the good of those who love him, who have been called according to his purpose. (vv. 26–28 NIV)

So keep praying—and know that God has always got your best interests at heart.

Be still.

When I first approached my dad about my Snow-Ball stand, he said no. Once again, my dad could see more than I could see (young people tend to see things only in the present; adults are pretty good at looking at the present *and* the future). It was time for me to take a moment and "be still." Once you tell God what you want and talk to Him about it, you might even take some steps toward making it happen. But if you encounter some resistance, there may be a reason why; it might be time to "be still" with your actions and think about the best ways to face your challenges.

Stay focused.

Have you ever heard the old saying, "You can't see the forest for the trees?" Well, I learned the meaning of that saying the hard way—except, actually, I guess it was the other way around: I couldn't see the tree.

Once I was driving to church, and I saw a huge flock of birds in a field. I wanted to jump right into the middle of the flock and take a selfie (wouldn't you?), so I swerved into the field. However, in my excitement, I was so focused on the birds that I didn't see a tree right in front of me.

And, as trees tend to do, it came out of nowhere. Then the inevitable happened.

Sitting in the field with my front bumper wrapped around a tree and birds flying all around me, I learned another important lesson: don't get so caught up in your plan that you can't see the big picture. God gave you eyes for a reason—use them.

THINK ABOUT IT

1. Is there a risk you're afraid to take? Why?
2. Go back and read 1 Samuel 17 in the Bible. How did David know he should take on Goliath?
3. If you could risk anything, knowing you wouldn't fail, what would it be?
4. Write about a time in your life when you took a small risk. How'd it turn out? Did it produce anything bigger?
5. Think about Bob Goff's advice: "If you want more faith, do more stuff." What might "doing more stuff" look like for you?
6. Being open, honest, and vulnerable can be a risk, but it's a risk that could pay off in ways you couldn't imagine. When in your life has being honest and vulnerable paid off for you? Were you surprised by the results?

Book Highlight #8

Jesus Wants to Save Christians by Rob Bell

Without *Jesus Wants to Save Christians, I would still think that being a Christian was all about being safe.*

This title is intriguing, isn't it? After all, Christians are supposed to be the ones who are already saved, right?

If you pick up this book, Rob Bell will definitely challenge your thinking, because he paints a picture of what can happen when Christians support the thinking, the behaviors, and the attitudes that our culture celebrates—and that Jesus came to deliver people from. Rob says that Jesus came to free us Christians, and when we oppress others under the guise of being a "Christian," we are binding them back to spiritual slavery; when we fail to be a light to the world, we drive those around us back into spiritual slavery. Jesus' ministry was about caring for those less fortunate—and Rob asserts that the American way of life is counterproductive to that message: "Could it be that all the harm we're seeking to be protected from is not nearly as destructive as the harm we are bringing upon ourselves?"[6]

Again, this is a book that'll challenge your way of thinking—this isn't always a bad thing. Encountering challenges is the only way we're going to grow and become more prepared to take on the other obstacles we'll face throughout our spiritual walk.

CHAPTER 9

SHINING

(NOW)

It does not do to dwell on
dreams and forget to live.

—J. K. ROWLING, *HARRY POTTER AND
THE SORCERER'S STONE*

SO I DECIDED TO SHINE . . .

When I went to the Passion Conference in Atlanta, Georgia, I heard a pastor named Carl Lentz from Hillsong Church in New York City speak. And he said something pretty insightful: "Jesus has done the work, He saved our lives, and we have a pretty clear call, which is to shine."

To me, shining is *doing*—it's taking the message of Jesus to the streets and letting others see why we have joy. Why we have hope. Why we have peace. Why we have love.

Lentz's message was clear: I needed to shine more.

Then, he encouraged us to remove the word *someday* from our vocabulary. "Do things *today*." He told us to occupy urgency. That's a great way to say "start now!"

So right after that, I decided to start. *That day*. I began with making a list of things I'd been putting off.

I love making lists. I've done this for as long as I can remember. All those lists of notes from sermons and books and classes at school and life lessons have gone into my toolbox. That day, I made a list of the things I needed to do in order to "occupy the streets," as Lentz put it, or to let Jesus shine through me with the light of the gospel.

My list included a book I was going to order, another I planned to read, a plumbing job I was going to get done, a porch I wanted to build for someone, and a conversation I needed to have with a friend.

Soon enough, over the course of a couple of weeks, I had the satisfaction of checking every item off the list. For a list nerd like me, there's no better feeling than making a list and then getting those things done.

The world loves to talk about and sing songs about shining. We all want to shine "someday." But God wants us to go out there and shine *now*. Whatever it is that we're putting off, we're missing an opportunity to show Jesus and to grow in Him.

Just Do It

Lentz's speech inspired me. What inspires you? Where do you look for inspiration?

Apparently, I am somewhat impressionable, so inspiration might come easily to me. One of my earliest inspirations occurred when I first saw the movie *The Lion King.* I'm not sure how old I was, but I'm hoping I was pretty young. This is another one of those stories handed down from my mom. She loves to tell how I was so inspired by Simba the lion that I wanted to be him. I would crawl around pretending to be a lion, roaring as loud as I could and even licking things. (Don't judge.)

Then another movie caught my attention. *All Dogs Go to Heaven* had me pretending I was a dog, and I would even play fetch with my family. I would bring things up to my mom or dad and get them to throw them so I could retrieve them.

I guess calling myself "easily inspired" might be putting it mildly, but as I got older, I did look for better things to inspire me than lions and dogs. (I knew I was a weird little kid, but I never really got the extent of *how* weird I was until typing this just now.)

More recently, people and books have inspired me more than anything else. I remember reading a book called *Born to Run* by Christopher McDougall. It's the fascinating, true story about the author living among the Tarahumara Indians in the Copper Canyon of Mexico. He learned the secrets of running from one of the tribesmen, all while training to run a fifty-mile race in that rugged terrain.

After I read this book, my whole thought process about running changed. First, I didn't wear shoes for months while running. (Or while doing almost anything else.) McDougall argues (pretty successfully, to me) that modern athletic shoes can sometimes do more harm than good to our feet. *Born to Run* shows how we as humans are all meant to run, and we can do it for joy instead of getting into shape or building stamina for a race.

My new love of running inspired me to start a running club. It was summertime, so I decided to try those weird shoes that look more like foot-gloves than anything else. I wasn't particularly good at running, but I was dedicated and ran every day. I felt like Forrest Gump. And my running club grew quickly— then the Louisiana heat started to kick in. And my running club died just as quickly as it had grown, but it was fun while it lasted. When school started back, to fill the void of my lost running club, I joined the school's cross-country team. Then, a lot like Forrest (if Forrest had thrown up and almost lost to an eleven-year-old at a cross-country meet), I just decided it was time to stop running. It was time. My feet thanked me, but I have to admit, I did look pretty awesome in those foot-glove shoes.

Besides running, I went through plenty of other "inspired" phases in high school. One phase I had was when I decided to write real, handwritten letters to people. It seemed to me that, with how connected we are digitally, we were losing the art of writing letters. There was something so different about writing on paper versus typing on a keyboard or the screen of a phone. I was reminded how significant and fun it felt to receive a real letter in the mail.

I began to write letters to all my friends and mail them, even though I saw these people at school every day. It didn't matter. The letters weren't that long, but they were in ink and in my not-so-great handwriting. They were original, made of paper, and could be held in somebody's hands or saved in a shoebox. There was something special about tangible items being delivered to those I loved.

Growing up, I guess I had this firecracker sort of mentality with inspiration. An idea would come with a short fuse, and then *boom*! Off I'd go, putting the idea into action and trying it out. I don't regret any of my attempts to shine (well, maybe the licking-things phase). Inspiration is the first step to allowing God to shine through you. There's so much to inspire each of us. Look around you. Maybe there's a teacher who makes an extra effort to motivate you. Maybe there's a song with just the words you need to hear. Maybe there's a sunset with the right colors to change your day. Inspiration is everywhere. Keep looking.

Uganda

Right after a crazy, inspirational summer came the fall of 2014, the beginning of my senior year of high school. I had several opportunities that inspired me that summer. Besides the Canada adventure, my family had hosted a Duck Commander cruise; I had gone on two mission trips to the Dominican Republic and Nicaragua; and I had attended summer camp at Camp Ch-Yo-Ca.

That fall our family received yet another invitation from Bob Goff—in an e-mail that was very Bob-like:

> Hey, if anyone from the Robertson family wants to go to Uganda, I'm going in a month.
>
> —Bob

Remember, it doesn't take much to inspire me. So right away I just knew, "Yes. I'm going."

At the time, I was reading Donald Miller's *A Million Miles in a Thousand Years*, so I was amped up and ready to live a great story. I vividly remember reading this line: "When we live a story, we are telling the people around us what we think is important."[1] And this is something I thought was very important. I was all in for Uganda, and anything else that might come my way.

I wanted to tell a better story.

"We live in a world where bad stories are told, stories that teach us life doesn't mean anything and that humanity has no great purpose," Don wrote in his book. "It's a good calling, then, to speak a better story. How brightly a better story shines."[2]

There's that word again. And, yes, I wanted to *shine*.

I accepted Bob's invitation, and after working things out with my school, on November 6, 2014, I left for a whirlwind, twelve-day trip. I met up with Bob in Pittsburgh, and then we flew to Uganda. When we arrived, we were going to visit the school he started years earlier, back when the LRA was still in control.

"LRA" stands for the "Lord's Resistance Army," which is a group of rebels that formed in northern Uganda in the mid-eighties. Over the years, this nightmarish group took many innocent lives; they even kidnapped children and forced them to fight in their army. Eventually the LRA was driven out of Uganda, but they still remain a terror in other parts of Africa.

While the LRA still controlled Uganda, Bob had the courage to start a school in the heart of the country. By 2014, the Restore School had been running for seven years, and every year Bob went back to Uganda to attend graduation. This was one of the reasons we were heading over there.

It took an entire day—twenty-four hours—and lots of stops to get to Entebbe, Uganda, but we made it. And I was ready for the adventure!

That night Bob had arranged for us to have supper with one of Uganda's Supreme Court justices, some judges, and other high-ranking officials. These were men Bob had been working with over the past several years to keep his school running. But meeting with those important men was just the beginning of our journey. We would eventually go to a tiny airport in the middle of nowhere and climb into a tiny bush plane held together by duct tape. The plane took us to the city of Gulu, where we visited a prison. The prison was a desolate, open structure with four walls, and it was crammed with people. This might have been the time to get a little nervous but, hey, I was with Bob.

The prison also had a Restore School operating inside it.

Bob and the group at Love Does have been very busy in Uganda, setting up schools and safe houses for exploited under-age girls, as well as a variety of justice programs supporting human rights.

In this prison, there were no cells. Just cardboard on the floor. No beds at all and no running water. (Well, they had some kind of running water, but it was too nasty to drink.) The people imprisoned there cooked chickens and goats and basically raised their own food, all while confined in four guarded walls, where they slept on rows of dirty cardboard mats. The only covering was on a little building that served as the infirmary.

And inside the walls was a small pavilion where they held school.

This prison was originally built for around three hundred people, but there were over eight hundred people living there when we visited. It was one of the saddest things I had ever seen.

Why was this prison so overcrowded? Well, Uganda has a pretty troubled legal system. While the country actually has a good police force, they don't have enough lawyers and judges to try every case. So if you get arrested, you're in quite a bit of trouble. There's no "innocent until proven guilty" in Uganda. And in America, if you're arrested and can make your bail, you can wait for your trial outside of jail. But Uganda doesn't have a bail system. If you're arrested there, you're put into jail and have to wait there for a trial.

Some of the people I encountered in this prison had never been tried. So, guilty or not, they'd been sitting in prison for years. *Waiting.*

Some were as young as fifteen years old. *Younger than me.*

This was one of the reasons Bob got involved. Since he's a lawyer, he could go to Uganda and actually try cases. At first he did that alone, but now he brings teams of lawyers with him. There are so many Ugandans awaiting trial that it takes more than one lawyer to get anything done. Bob says since he started bringing his team along, they have collectively cleared out four prisons.

Heaven's light is surely shining down on the work Bob is doing.

Besides attending the graduation, Bob's visit also included checking on the schools to see how things were going. He talked to the teachers and then talked to the prison warden to see how the students were doing. I stood in awe as Bob worked his way through people and their problems. All the while, Bob shone.

Another stop was to a convent to visit Sister Rosemary. Sister Rosemary Nyirumbe is pretty famous, and it was an honor to meet her. *Time* magazine listed her as one of the one hundred most influential people in the world in 2014.[3] There was a Netflix documentary about her called *Sewing Hope*, describing her work with women who had been held captive and abused by the LRA. She is part of the Sisters of the Sacred Heart of Jesus missionary congregation based in Juba, South Sudan.

Bob and I visited the Sisters' Saint Monica campus in Gulu. At the campus, women learn how to become self-reliant while discovering hope and peace. Sister Rosemary teaches these women skills, such as how to make their own clothes, grow their own food, and learn different trades. She also shows them how to show mercy.

Bob and Sister Rosemary worked together to start a kindergarten at this nunnery, and seeing this school was such an amazing experience. The kids all wore pink shirts and looked adorable. There was an extraordinary sense of tranquility and peace there, with all the kids and nuns walking around. All I could think of was how Sister Rosemary was shining and making such a difference in the lives of those kids.

Our next trip was to visit another school, which had been started for former witch doctors. After going from prisoners to kindergarteners to witch doctors, my head was spinning.

This is an incredible story Bob is living, I kept repeating to myself.

Bob Goff discovered that witch doctors actually conducted child sacrifices. So, once again, he took action and got a law passed that made child sacrifice punishable by death. Then he managed to get all the witch doctors in the country to meet at one place. When they showed up, Bob greeted them, along with the Supreme Court justice, and warned them if they sacrificed any children, the authorities would catch them and try them— and the witch doctors would be hanged.

Then Bob told the witch doctors that if they wanted to change their lives and get an education, he had a school where they could go. They could learn how to read and write. Two of the textbooks taught are *Love Does* and the Bible.

There were so many adventures packed into that one trip. The whole time we were in Uganda, I was reminded over and over again of a quote from Bob's book:

"Love is never stationary."[4]

Bob was demonstrating love by *doing*. And I was learning too. I'm so glad I decided to go for it and take Bob up on his invitation. God showed me the shining faces of many in a country so full of desperation and hopelessness—all because one man and an order of nuns decided to let God shine through them.

The glow—the shine that comes from serving others and God—was on the faces of Bob and Sister Rosemary, but it really was just a reflection of the One who could offer real hope when it seemed none was possible.

Put a Ring on It

Back at home, I was jumping into another sort of adventure. Decisions don't have to take a long time, I'd learned—even the important ones. That same fall of 2014, it was time to decide where things were going with Mary Kate. That summer our relationship had been on an adventure too. We had traveled quite a bit on a school trip and to Canada, so we had gotten to know each other really well. I knew I loved her.

So then what? So now what happens?

I knew the story I wanted to start telling, and I knew Mary Kate was an important part of it.

I want to make something clear to you. I didn't decide it was time to marry Mary Kate because I had a crush on her and couldn't stand being apart from her. No, at this time we were actually working hard on our relationship. We had been together long enough and gone through enough challenges that I was able to see something that my parents, uncles and aunts, and grandparents had taught me: keeping this relationship going is going to be hard. You see, given enough time and circumstances, any relationship will get strained. Mary Kate and I had reached the point where the gushy, romantic feelings weren't the only thing there. We had experienced what it means to love someone, even when the conditions aren't perfect. My proposal to Mary Kate wasn't topping off a relationship high that needed an ending. I knew it was way deeper than that.

And I knew this for sure: we could get through the tough times.

Real life can be tough, and the rush of new love or young love never lasts.

C. S. Lewis wrote in *Mere Christianity* that love was different from "being in love." True love isn't a feeling, but a "deep unity, maintained by the will and deliberately strengthened by habit; reinforced by (in Christian marriages) the grace which both partners ask, and receive, from God."[5] I knew that the feelings Mary Kate and I had for each other were feelings of love. I also knew that we could come together, keep our promises, and create a life in which we experience a deeper sense of love through Christ.

Mary Kate was confident of who she was. I knew if we broke up, she would be fine. She had God, and that was all she needed. I had God, and that was all I needed. So we were both whole people, and that's what we'd both been looking for. When I found her, she was already this whole person who could handle herself and who didn't need me.

I could see her spending seventy or eighty years *not* needing me but remaining at my side. I could see the two of us living lives of doing and going and loving while also seeking God and admitting we need Him.

So on my nineteenth birthday on October 11, 2014, I asked my best friend to marry me.

My parents and both sets of grandparents had married at a young age and were examples of how relationships could and should work.

For me, I didn't have to go to college first or experience more life. I was ready.

The order in which you live your life isn't as important as living it with all your heart. Don't put off things like a life-changing trip because the timing doesn't seem perfect. Don't postpone doing something remarkable because it feels scary and tiring or because you're young.

Accomplishing great things—shining in a dark world—means not being afraid to take action. If something honors God, follows His laws, and brings more love to the world . . . go for it!

To Wait or Not to Wait

Before we leave the subject of shining, I want to talk about one more thing. Knowing when to get up and go can be a serious dilemma for most people. Even though I am a "get up and go" person, I have learned the value in waiting. In the book *Oh, the Places You'll Go!* by Dr. Seuss, there's a place he simply calls "The Waiting Place":

> Waiting for a train to go or a bus to come,
> or a plane to go or the mail to come,
> or the rain to go or the phone to ring,
> or the snow to snow or

waiting around for a Yes or a No
or waiting for their hair to grow.[6]

Waiting is a part of life, and it's not always a bad thing. In fact, we're warned in the Bible to wait on the Lord, to be more concerned with His timing than our own, to listen for His answers. So, when you're given the opportunity to "go for it," don't forget to talk to God about it first. Remember the five points in the last chapter about God's will (pages 140–143)? Keep those in mind when opportunities come up, and you'll do just fine.

THINK ABOUT IT

1. Make a list of five simple things you've wanted to do, but for some reason, you've put off.
2. What are some things that inspired you as a younger kid? What inspires you today?
3. Make a list of three big dreams you hope to accomplish. What can you do now to get these dreams started?
4. Being patient and taking action seem to be opposite activities. Which one is easier for you?
5. There are many verses in the Bible that tell us to wait. Look up Isaiah 40:31. Read it and list four things that will happen when you wait on the Lord.

Book Highlight #9

Unleash! by Perry Noble

Without Unleash!, *I would still be picking a number under one hundred.*

It was a last-minute decision to go to NewSpring Church in South Carolina, and that was when I was introduced to Pastor Perry Noble. That, in itself, tells me that God is looking out for me. Perry Noble is a great warrior for God. He has a church he pastors, a family he loves, Twitter and blog followers to keep up with, books he's written—I could go on and on about the good stuff he does. In his messages, Perry challenges Christians to be bold in fully embracing the exciting adventure God has called us to.

Unleash! is about answering this question: are you ready to unleash all the life God has created you to live? Perry says God longs to unleash His full measure of power in our lives so that He can fill us with passion and purpose. But sometimes, we actually hold ourselves back from feeling God's power. Too often we let the things of our past—fear, anger, bitterness, worry, and doubt—shackle our progress. Rather than focusing on how Christ redeemed us, we allow ourselves to be identified by all the negative parts of our past that shouldn't hold power over us. We need to remember that we are not who our past says we are, and we are not who the enemy says we are. We are who God and His Word say that we are.

I know I've said this before, but this book will change your life!

CHAPTER 10

FAILING

(AND GETTING BACK UP)

I know that fear is an obstacle for some
people, but it is an illusion to me. . . . Failure
always made me try harder next time.

—MICHAEL JORDAN

SO I FAILED . . .

FAILED BECAUSE OF UNSUPPORTIVE FAMILY AND
FIANCÉE

This was my journal entry after a failed experiment.

Actually, I have a long list of failures over my lifetime. When you're willing to try new things, you're bound to miss the mark a few times (or, if you're me, lots of times).

So here's what happened with the Uberman Sleep Schedule.

It started the way so many things do—I read a book. This one was called *The 4-Hour Body*. Now, wait until the end before you make any judgments, okay? The author concluded that some study on sleep said that all you really need is two hours of sleep a day if you can go into your REM state immediately. The book shows how you can train yourself to go into this REM sleep if you only sleep twenty minutes every four hours. So basically, every four hours, you take a twenty-minute nap. Day and night, for the whole twenty-four-hour cycle. Every four hours, it's nap time. (The scientific term for this is *polyphasic sleep*.)

This looked fascinating, so I decided to try it. I set my alarm, and every four hours, I would take a twenty-minute nap. Or at least try to.

I took some notes in my journal when I did this. Here's an excerpt:

The first day I am already tired but I should get used to it soon.

I am doing this because my life physically has gotten out of control. I talk about having vision about what you want your life to look like, but I am not doing this with my own body. So here we go.

It is 2:24 A.M. I am listening to Train and about to start my homework.

Life right now is the perfect time to do it. I am not in school. (Side note: I was finishing my senior year on an independent work program through my high school.) I have no schedule I need to be on except the one I put on myself. So I am going to make it count.

The first day, I thought, *Yeah, this is going pretty well!* I stayed up all night and was getting so much done because I had much more time in the day.

Then day two came. And it was pretty rough. My body started to feel strange. I felt a bit sick and dizzy and bizarre.

By day three, I felt like I was dying.

I was trying my best to stay on schedule, drinking coffee and watching the time. But here's the thing: it was super inconvenient to everyone around me. I'd be in the middle of a conversation and suddenly break it off, saying, "Uh, excuse me. I need to go take a nap."

By day four, my body was starting to adjust to it. I would take a nap at 3:00 A.M., so around 2:55 A.M. I would start getting tired, and by 3:00 A.M.I'd be out. If I missed a nap, then I would be totally messed up, since it takes forever to get back to the schedule. By day five or six, I didn't even think of sleeping. I mean, I wasn't consumed with *when* I could sleep. I was adjusting to it.

Everybody thought I was crazy. "John Luke," they'd say, "what are you doing? This is *not* working."

Yeah, I was walking around like an extra on *The Walking Dead*. But sometimes you have to try new things, right?

My family . . . they weren't helpful at all. My mother said it was a little comparable to a baby needing a nap every few hours.

"John Luke, normal life doesn't work like this. You can't just go and take a nap whenever you have to."

Mary Kate was annoyed with me because I kept having to take a nap. I was annoyed with Mary Kate because she wasn't. I had eight more hours in the day to go on all kinds of adventures while she was wasting her time sleeping. I'm not gonna lie, it was really lonely at 2:00 A.M. Yes, sure, everybody in the country was sleeping at this time, but still.

My journal continued:

Uberman Sleep Day 2
   I have successfully had 4 naps.

There's a break in the journal. I might have been too tired to write anything. Then there's large print written sideways on the page:

FAILED BECAUSE OF UNSUPPORTIVE FAMILY AND FIANCÉE

Mary Kate saw this and added her thoughts:

And it was not a bright idea.

So, yes, sure—I didn't quite succeed with the Uberman Sleep Schedule. But since then, whenever I want to go to sleep or take a nap, I'm out. I can fall asleep *anywhere*.

You could consider the experiment a big failure, but it had come from one simple question: *Why not?* I had followed through on that thought and had a new experience, just as when I went to Canada or bought the building.

Why not? is a very legitimate question. One reason many decide not to follow through on the question is *you might fail*. It might end up being a dumb idea. Your family might make fun of you and repeatedly tell you, "That's ridiculous." But I know one thing: people have said that about any number of great ideas in the past. I'm totally willing to take a chance and look like a fool. Who knows when something might turn out to actually work!

Hope in Failing

When you look at some of the most successful people of all time and read their backstories, you soon realize that almost every single one of them experienced a loss or felt the sting of defeat on their journeys.

J. K. Rowling was a single mother barely managing to get by and living on welfare when she started to write a book. Dozens of publishers rejected her first book.

Elvis Presley got turned down at an early audition. Not only that, but the teenager was told to stick with driving a truck since he was never going to make it as a singer.

Michael Jordan wasn't considered a great basketball player when he was younger. His older brother, Larry, was taller and better. After Michael tried out for the varsity basketball team in tenth grade, his name didn't appear on the team roster.

Bill Gates dropped out of Harvard and started a business with a fellow young entrepreneur. They created a processing service called Traf-O-Data, which didn't work and they couldn't sell.

Harrison Ford could only get minor roles and got booted from his young talent program as he was trying to get into acting. When all the doors seemed shut, Ford supported his family as a carpenter, even building stages and sets for TV shows and movies.

Here's an example I really like: Thomas Edison was considered dumb by his schoolteachers, got fired from his first two jobs, and made over a thousand unsuccessful attempts while trying to invent one very specific thing. Who tries a thousand times? Thomas Edison did.

Abraham Lincoln? Goodness—there's not enough space

here to list all his failures. He's got a pretty big laundry list of failures: failing in business, losing when he ran for state legislature, having a nervous breakdown, and being defeated when running for speaker of the state legislature (and then elector, and then Congress, and then land officer in his home state, and then US Senate, and then . . .).

Whew. It's discouraging just writing about Lincoln's failures!

But I bet you know the outcomes to those failures. See if you can match the "fail-er" with what he or she eventually contributed to the world. If these people had stopped and stayed stuck in their defeat, the world wouldn't have:

- *Harry Potter*
- "Jailhouse Rock" and "Heartbreak Hotel"
- The Chicago Bulls' six championships
- Microsoft
- Han Solo and Indiana Jones
- The light bulb
- The Emancipation Proclamation and the Gettysburg Address

All these people and their stories are part of history. It's easy for us to take them for granted.

The truth is that every single one of these people faced a time when they were discouraged, let down, and even broken. There were moments when they could have done the safe and easy thing: *stop*.

Yet they teach us that success comes *after* you've been knocked down and have picked yourself up again.

In reality, it can be hard to actually do that. It's easy to tweet a motivational slogan. It's difficult to actually go out and live it.

Sailing Takes Me Away . . .

This past year on our family beach trip to Alabama, I decided to take our sailboat out with my cousin Reed one afternoon. By this time, I had taken the boat out a few times (on a small pond) and watched a lot of YouTube videos on how to operate the boat. So I was basically an expert.

Reed and I looked out over the rocky seas and decided we could do it. We waved goodbye to our moms, aunts, uncles, and grandparents, who were all on the beach ready to call for help if they noticed anything amiss, and we pushed our way into the choppy water. Within minutes we were sailing, and our family on the shore got smaller and smaller. The sky grew darker, and the wind picked up. Suddenly we both heard a *pop*. There are three lines that hold the mast up, and one had broken.

We were terrified!

Fortunately, I felt a shudder and the line swung over right in front of my face (thank You, Lord), and I caught it. If we had lost that line, we would have been in big trouble. But even though I caught the broken line, it still wasn't attached. That was a problem. Turning left meant another line breaking, and turning right meant going farther out to sea. At that point, going out to sea was our only option. Before we left the shore, Mom told me she would call for help if I wasn't back in an hour. I began to wonder if she had made the call yet. Eventually, we used the

YOUNG AND BEARDLESS

only thing available—zip ties and duct tape (never leave home without it). Once we attached the line, we were able to turn the boat toward the shore.

Even in the terror of the moment, I realized something important. We cannot let fear overcome us. Fear is an emotion that can keep you from moving forward. Courage is choosing not to give into that emotion. (I'm sure I read that somewhere.) I knew we had to keep fighting.

As the waves grew around us, I understood why the apostle Peter was terrified when he tried walking to Jesus on the water. Sometimes our troubles look like they will overwhelm us. Peter failed at walking on water and was left with only one other option besides drowning: calling out to Jesus.

With Jesus there is always another option.

Jesus immediately reached out and grabbed [Peter]. "You have so little faith," Jesus said. "Why did you doubt me?" (Matthew 14:31)

While our situation was not one of little faith (it was maybe poor decision-making), the only way forward was to have faith and trust God despite our mistake. It was either option A or B:

Option A: Sit down, put my head in my hands, and end up in South America (or worse).
Option B: Cry out to God and ask for His help and keep working.

Unlike Peter, Jesus didn't physically grab us, but there is no doubt in my mind that there was a power that helped Reed and me get back to shore. My mom was minutes away from calling the Coast Guard.

The reason I'm telling you this is definitely *not* to encourage dangerous sailing adventures. (Really. Just be smart, guys.) I'm telling you this story because no matter how careless *or* careful you are, sometimes you're going to make mistakes. But *when* you fail (not *if*), you can make a choice to let it swallow you, drown you, stop you—or you can cry out to God for the strength to get out of it. With God, you will always get through it.

Hang in there. Turn to Jesus, and don't let your failures overcome you when it's all on the line.

The Dark Side of the Moon

I've shared some stories about Papaw Howard. It's easy to look at him as only a successful entrepreneur and businessman. But like so many I've mentioned in this chapter, Papaw Howard also experienced some failures.

One of my favorite Papaw Howard stories concerning failure is the one about the fast-food business he opened.

In the 1960s, Alton Howard and some partners decided to open a fast-food restaurant called Moon Burger. The building looked like a spaceship. To place an order, the customers would have to walk up a long set of steps to reach the window. There was no inside service—it was strictly takeout. This wasn't the best on rainy days. Problem number one.

Wanting to capitalize on the name "Moon Burger," Papaw thought it would be fun to have a robot take the orders and bring them down to customers who wanted to use the drive-through. This presented problem number two: the robot was on a conveyor belt fifteen feet in the air that came down from a "spaceship" forty feet away. It sounds great, right? But the robot had to move slowly in order to keep the drinks from tipping. This meant the robot could only serve five or six drive-through customers during the busiest service time—the lunch hour.

Moon Burger was a fun concept, but it certainly wasn't *fast* food. It lasted only a few months before it was declared a disaster. Even the best businessman couldn't turn that around to be profitable.

If only Papaw Howard could see what they're doing with robots these days. Who knows what ideas he might come up with?

The School

Remember the school building I planned on turning into a recovery home? The one I proudly announced in front of fifteen thousand students at Liberty University? The thing I tried to do because I wanted more faith?

I wish I could tell you that building is on its way to being the recovery house I dreamed it to be and announced it was going to be, but I can't. Because of circumstances out of my control, the building never became mine. I was so excited about the possibilities that I jumped the gun and make the announcement before I should have.

"Okay, we'll put it on hold," I said when I was first told it was not going to happen. "We'll wait for things to calm down, and then we'll go back with an offer, and the owners will reconsider it."

But after a few weeks, it was clear it wasn't going to happen.

My dreams for doing something big had been defeated. It felt like all the time and effort and ideas and plans were just a waste of time. And, to make matters worse, I had announced it to thousands of people.

I tried to put Bob Goff's "love does" principle into action, and it seemed to backfire on me. The only thing left was to learn the lessons God would teach me. One lesson is a hard one: even though love does a lot of things, not all of those things will work out—or maybe not the way you intended.

So, my choices were now in front of me. *How will failure affect me? Will I be resentful?* I had shared a dream in front of thousands. *How embarrassing is this whole thing?* I was going to look stupid. All those who already thought my idea was dumb would only be nodding in a know-it-all, we-told-you-so way.

Am I going to wallow around in this, or am I going to move on?

Keep reading. There were more lessons for me to learn.

This Thing Is Not Going to Break You

Let me tell you about someone I recently met who saw the face of hate in this world—the face of evil—and was given a choice. Would she remain broken? Or could she show the beauty of God's grace by moving on?

On July 20, 2012, just moments after a midnight showing of *The Dark Knight Rises* began at a movie theater near Denver, a man walked to the front of the theater and began shooting. Twelve people were killed, and more than seventy people were injured that night.

Many of us remember when that happened. We watched as the killer went on trial and was eventually condemned to twelve life sentences and the maximum 3,318 years in prison for his horrific actions.

One of the seventy people injured that night was a young woman named Bonnie Kate Pourciau. During the gunfire, she felt a big bang on her left knee, as if a two-by-four had suddenly struck it. She then ducked behind a seat and curled up in a ball, taking her friend's hand and pulling her down beside her.

Something incredible happened at that moment. While everything around Bonnie Kate was crazy, she says she felt something totally unexpected.

Peace.

"I've never felt the amount of peace that I did in that moment when I thought I wasn't going to make it," Bonnie Kate said later in an interview. "I just felt like God wrapped me up, and I wasn't scared. It's weird, but in the midst of all that horror, God was really near to me."[1]

Because of the knee injury, she couldn't run to an exit, so she crawled out army style until a man came by and helped her. Once she was out of the theater, she could see her knee was gushing blood from a gunshot. The ambulances were all full, so she rode to the hospital in a police car.

Since the injury, she's endured many major surgeries, including stem-cell treatments to save her leg. She still walks with crutches and deals with daily pain.

While sitting in the hospital recovering from this terrible, life-changing event, Bonnie Kate had the same two options I had after the building disaster (and that you have after any failure): Do we trust God and know He loves us and has a plan for everything, or do we choose to let the darkness defeat us?

It certainly would have been easy to understand if Bonnie

Kate had been angry at God and bitter about what had happened. But instead she felt grateful to be alive. So while bedridden in the hospital with excruciating pain, she made the choice to forgive the man who had done this to her.

In an interview, Bonnie Kate said something remarkable about the shooter: "I felt so much for this man who is so broken, who doesn't know the hope that we Christians have, who doesn't understand the mercy of God, and who doesn't know Jesus."[2]

These are words that many would find hard to say. But as a Christian she knew there was more to the story. She knew that young man must have been deeply broken to hurt so many others, and that he needed Jesus.

Her story didn't end there.

Two years after the shooting, Max Zoghbi, who had been by Bonnie Kate's side during her recovery, helped mend some of the broken pieces inside of her with a gift. Max was a filmmaker, but more importantly, he loved Bonnie Kate. He patiently pursued her and eventually won her heart, which led to a surprising and epic marriage proposal.

The twist? He proposed in a movie theater.

Since Max is a creative guy who loves to document the world through recording it on camera, he filmed the whole experience and made a beautiful twenty-five-minute film of the footage called *Wildflower*. In the description of the video on YouTube, this is what Max wrote about Bonnie Kate:

> Wildflower. That is what comes to mind when I consider my bride Bonnie Kate. Much like a wildflower, she is the strongest and bravest person I know with unmatched, unintentional

beauty and fragility both inside and out. Choosing to grow and persevere even in the harshest of seasons and circumstances, Bonnie Kate shines brightly through the darkness and chooses to accept joy every step of the long, painful and seemingly endless way. We know that this long suffering, this present darkness is for an unfathomably greater good to come, and this film is a small glimpse into wrestling with that reality.[3]

Fast forward to 2014, when Mary Kate started following Bonnie Kate on Instagram. Mary Kate loved her pictures and story, but she didn't know her personally. Mary Kate and I found out that Max and Bonnie Kate lived in Louisiana too, so we decided to contact them to see if Max would film our wedding. We were thrilled when he said yes. Before the wedding, Mary Kate and I were in Baton Rouge, and we knew Max and Bonnie Kate lived there. We got in touch with them to see if they could join us for lunch. Another yes, and we were soon friends. We were just starting our journey to meet couple-friends (trust me, it's easier to hang out with couples when you're married), and it was fun to meet another couple who had a lot in common with us.

Max and Bonnie Kate are incredible examples of two people the world could have broken, but instead, they choose to embody love and joy in their lives. Both of them will tell you they're able to make those choices not because they're relying on their own strengths, but because they're leaning on God.

At some point in our lives, we all will fall. We will encounter trials and tribulations. But we have to remember something Joseph told his brothers many years ago: "You intended to harm me, but God intended it all for good. He brought me to this position so I could save the lives of many people" (Genesis 50:20).

A hard lesson to learn firsthand, but an important one nonetheless: hardships, obstacles, even tragedies can be used for God's glory—but only if we allow them to be.

Admitting Failure

Unlike my sailboat story and my building episode, Bonnie Kate did nothing to create the situation she suffered through. She is destined to a life of physical suffering because of someone else's choices. But when you're the author of your own failure, it can be, well, embarrassing.

It's fun to have your family sit on the beach as you sail smoothly across the water. But when they spend an hour in terror wondering if you're going to make it home safely, all because of *your* poor judgment, it's not fun at all. And it's one thing to stand up in front of a crowd of young people and proudly announce the plans of something remarkable you want to do. It's quite another to go back and stand before them and admit to failing. But this was what happened when I gave a second speech at Liberty University on April 24, 2015.

At the time, I didn't quite know what to think. On one hand, it felt cathartic and authentic to do this in front of everybody. Yet afterward, I saw people on Twitter and other social media saying things like, "That was so pointless," and "Why would he go up there and say that?" Some were saying, "Why did he just go up in front of us and tell us he failed?"

They just didn't seem to see the hand of God in this story.

I told everybody about the dream I'd had and about sharing

this dream in a previous speech at the school. Then I explained how I didn't get the building after all. (By the way, I didn't accept the $50,000 from Sean Hannity when I discovered that the project wouldn't work out.)

"It was bad," I told the crowd. "I thought, *Well, God is teaching me a lesson.* I realized that I always need to make sure a deal is done before talking about it."

I went on to explain the strange aftermath.

"So I was mad. At myself and even at God, because I thought the enemy had won and God didn't help me. I believed I had failed.

"Then last night I got a call. A storm hit Louisiana yesterday, with seventy-mile-per-hour winds. One wall of the school building I wanted to buy had collapsed. The building received extensive damage. When I heard this, all I could see was God protecting me from disaster. Just as Jesus told Peter after Peter walked on the water, I heard God saying, 'Why did you doubt me?'" And then I finally saw the result of my lesson.

I had more faith.

This was what I wanted to share with everybody when I gave that talk at Liberty, even if some people thought my admission was worthless. Fortunately, not everybody believed being vulnerable was a dumb idea. My mentors Jerry Falwell Jr., David Nasser, and Bob Goff all thought it was the right move.

Sharing our failures with others can help us leave those failures behind and keep moving forward. There's a great line from *The Hobbit* where Bilbo Baggins says, "'Go back?' he thought. 'No good at all! Go sideways? Impossible! Go forward? Only thing to do! On we go!'"[4]

Like Bilbo, sometimes all we can do in life is not look back and not head sideways, but keep walking on the road in front of us.

Planted Along a Riverbank

The great author Mark Twain had experienced many failures. He was a sick child growing up, made some money piloting a Mississippi riverboat, then lost everything he had trying a get-rich-quick scheme in the silver mines.

And the thing he was best at? Writing stories. And he only did that so he could eat.

It's no secret that Twain was a brilliant writer and story-teller, but he was a terrible businessman. He invested a ton of money in a groundbreaking automatic typesetting machine, but, as happens so often in business, another machine cornered the market. Twain's investment went belly-up. And ten years after publishing *The Adventures of Huckleberry Finn*, Mark Twain declared bankruptcy.

Yet Twain never let his failures keep him from trying again.

Perhaps Twain's life motto can be summed up in this *Huckleberry Finn* line: "The average man don't like trouble and danger."[5] He's saying that average people don't step out and try. They don't take chances. They don't want to venture into the unknown simply because many are afraid of the troubles to come. They don't want more faith.

One of the most helpful things we can realize is that we can't rely on our own talents and abilities in order to succeed—we have to have help. Recognizing we can't do this alone should take the pressure off of us because we have help! Jeremiah told us what happens when we accept the help God offers:

177

But blessed are those who trust in the LORD and have made the LORD their hope and confidence. They are like trees planted along a riverbank, with roots that reach deep into the water. Such trees are not bothered by the heat or worried by long months of drought. Their leaves stay green, and they never stop producing fruit. (Jeremiah 17:7–8)

I always want to trust the Lord and to remain strong when tough days come—and I will remain strong, if I continue to look to Him for help. At the end of my life, I want to be able to say, as Huckleberry Finn does, "I do not wish any reward but to know I have done the right thing."[6]

THINK ABOUT IT

1. Name a time when you faced failure. How did you handle it?
2. Are you someone who easily admits a mistake, or it is hard for you to own up to your faults?
3. You've probably heard someone say that "it's the hard times that make us grow." What does that mean to you?
4. First Peter 4:12 says, "Dear friends, don't be surprised at the fiery trials you are going through, as if something strange were happening to you." Why do you think most people are surprised when hard times come?
5. Mark Twain said the average man doesn't like danger. Do you agree?
6. Looking forward is the best way to move past a failure or a mistake. Can you think of someone you know who moved passed a mistake and on to something great?
7. Do want more faith? What do you need to do to have more faith?

Book Highlight #10:

The New Rules for Love, Sex, and Dating by Andy Stanley

Without The New Rules, *Mary Kate and I would still be fighting.*

YOUNG AND BEARDLESS

Andy Stanley is the founder of North Point Ministries based in Atlanta, Georgia. His ministry includes six churches in the Atlanta area and about thirty churches around the world. When Mary Kate and I were engaged, I wanted to find a book that would help me be the best husband I could be. Andy's publisher asked me to do an early review of this book, and it came to me at the perfect time.

Andy Stanley challenges our generation to change the way we date and think about forming long-term, successful relationships. He warns that our oversexualized culture can never deliver the satisfaction it promises, so we have to stop looking in all the wrong places for the right relationships.

In his introduction, he points out that all of us are exceptional, but we're not exceptions. This means that all of us have a story, but everyone's stories are similar. And as a pastor, Stanley has heard most kinds of stories before. In chapter one, he says you can't find the best person to marry if you're the wrong person yourself, so the change starts with you.

I put this book in the "Failure" section because we have all had relationships fail. This book offers some handy tools to help you break the cycle of poor relationships.

CHAPTER 11

GOING

(ON A JOURNEY)

May the wind under your wings bear you
where the sun sails and the moon walks.

—J. R. R. TOLKIEN, *THE HOBBIT*

SO I WENT ON A JOURNEY . . .

Every great story is about a journey. Many stories describe the
journeys of adventure the characters are taking. The Lord
of the Rings series is about Frodo and Sam's trek to Mount Doom
to throw the "One Ring" into the fiery chasm. *The Adventures of
Huckleberry Finn* is all about a kid and his friend floating down
the Mississippi River. The recent bestselling Young Adult novel
and movie *The Fault in Our Stars*, by John Green, is about two
teens in love going to visit an author in Amsterdam. We can't
get enough of stories about people leaving their homes to go
somewhere.

If you haven't yet read *Pilgrim's Progress* by John Bunyan, get ready because you probably will. It's usually on an English reading list at some point in high school or college. And it's about just that: a pilgrim making progress toward a destination. The main character, Christian, starts out on a pilgrimage to the Celestial City. The story is an allegory symbolizing a Christian's walk with God. There's a line in the story that talks about how it's hard to see the purpose in wanderings until the journey is over.

In great stories, the heroes always get lost and trapped and chased on their odyssey. All along, they are growing, figuring out their journey's purpose—just as we're doing every single day of our lives.

Getting Out of Dodge

After everything that had happened with the building, I realized I needed to focus my attention on something else. One day I woke up with a simple solution: *man, you need to get out of town.*

So I decided to text a new friend I'd met at an event. His name is Shawn, and he was on fire for the Lord. Shawn once told me he knew Francis Chan, and I told him I'd love to meet Chan one day, so Shawn gave me some advice: "If you ever come to San Francisco, you can run into him. You'll be able to catch him in my restaurant, where he has breakfast." During our quick encounter at the event, I didn't know Shawn was an amazing chef, but the whole eat-at-my-restaurant-and-meet-Chan thing seemed promising.

So I texted him: "Hey, man, something happened. I just need to get out of town. Can I come to San Francisco?"

Shawn texted back, "Yeah, I'll put you in the house." I

thought, *How nice of the guy to let me stay with him.* So I left on a Friday to go to San Francisco. I arrived, with no plans or itinerary other than connecting with this guy I'd met once and hoping to somehow meet Francis Chan. Shawn picked me up and brought me to "the house." I'd assumed that meant, you know, a home that he lived in by himself. It turned out to be a recovery house for ex-convicts and drug addicts.

It's called Bayview House, and it's part of Project Bayview—an amazing program that helps people coming out of broken situations. The goal is to provide "instant brotherhood, leadership development, mentorship, housing, career development, work, and fun."[1]

I discovered that Francis Chan had helped start Project Bayview. I also found out that the place he ate breakfast every morning was the restaurant at the bottom of this building. So I thought, *Why not?* and settled into the house to stay for a couple of nights.

Little did I know, I'd entered an episode of *Breaking Bad.*

One of my housemates was going to jail. Let's just call him Jesse for now. The technical charge was evading arrest. But he was evading the police because of a meth deal he'd been involved in that went bad. Jesse was arrested and sent to jail. Then, while out on bail and awaiting trial, he gave himself to God and completely changed his life. For the last month, as he waited to go back to jail and serve out his sentence, he had been living in Bayview House.

Clearly God was doing great things in very tough, very real situations. And it got even more real when I was out riding with Shawn one day. We saw a group of people standing on the side of the road, so Shawn stopped the car to get out and talk with them. He told me they were part of a gang that had experienced three deaths only a week earlier. Three of these men's friends, brothers, and sons had been gunned down in a drive-by shooting. Only one man had survived.

Naturally, I didn't want to get out of the car at first. But then I remembered something Shawn had told me right after I came to town: "You don't have to relate. You just have to love."

So we got out of the car and went over to pray for these guys. They were part of a gang, and some were killers themselves. All the more reason to ask the Lord to give them wisdom and keep them safe.

Ministries like Shawn's are here to show God's love to people who are living in all kinds of rough situations. Shawn wants these guys to know God and experience *that* kind of high—*that* kind of acceptance.

Back in the house, I noticed that every morning my housemate "Jesse" would get up and read his Bible, and then go out and help people. He would always share the gospel and tell them what had happened in his life. I decided to join him on his daily rounds, which started each day by going downstairs for breakfast. I kept my eyes peeled to see if Francis Chan would show up. I didn't know if he was in the city—or even in the country. Thankfully, after a couple days, Chan walked through the door.

"Would you like to sit?" I said.

Finally! I greeted him and told him my name, and then shared why I was there.

"I've just been hanging out, waiting for you."

You can imagine he was a bit surprised (at least, I hope it was surprise and not alarm), but he graciously replied with an "Okay."

"Would you like to talk?" I asked.

"Yes, we can talk."

So we had breakfast that morning and talked for an hour. The following morning we talked again briefly.

I really shouldn't say that we talked. I tried *not* to talk. I tried to listen. I couldn't write fast enough while taking notes on the things he said.

The first thing I noticed about Francis Chan was his humility. He would ask me a lot of questions, which I tried to answer quickly. I didn't want to take up our time hearing myself talk. I was there to listen to him.

The conversation consisted of many things, books being one of them, of course. We spoke about a few controversial books recently published by Christian authors. He also gave me an idea for a future book that I'd love to write one day (stay tuned).

Then he gave me a list that seemed like an invitation into another adventure.

"I'm going to give you the names of different people," he told me. "Go out and find these people and spend a couple of days with them, just like you're doing with me. Learn from them and watch how they do things. See what their views are and how they approach the world."

Chan wrote a list of very interesting people and gave it to me. It was like a map to the stars someone gives you in Hollywood, except these were spiritual stars. They were warriors in the great spiritual battle—people who have been traveling the pilgrim's path for a long time.

One of the names on this list was Tim Keller.

"Watch him make decisions," Chan said. "You need to be there when he makes one to watch and learn how he thinks through, plans, and decides. To see how logical he is and how carefully he thinks things through—not only his sermons but his actions."

Another name was Mike Bickle, the man who started the International House of Prayer.

"Find Mike, watch how faithful he is, and pray with him."

"Study the Bible with John Piper in the morning," Chan said. "Then watch how he puts what he studied into action."

Chan told me that his mentor was K. P. Yohannan, the founder and president of Gospel for Asia. Chan told me Yohannan is in a foreign country starting churches right now.

Each person he listed had some incredible trait. It reminded me of an old classic movie called *The Magnificent Seven*, where seven men are called to help a village, each for a different reason, and each bringing their own unique talent to the mix. Chan admitted he didn't always agree with some of the people on his list from a theological perspective, but nevertheless they were leaders to learn from. (This was amazing insight. Too many times we think if we don't agree with someone, we have nothing to learn from them.)

Ultimately, Chan's message was this: "Just go. Just drive around and find these people. Learn from them. Let them show you more about the God we serve." Learning from them, Chan said, would help change my world. After all, *they're* helping to change the world.

Who says you and I can't be one of those names someone scribbles on a piece of paper one day? Why can't we strive to be the sort of person that someone would actively seek out in order to ask questions and gain some of the wisdom we've picked up along the journey?

I think that's a pretty awesome goal to aspire to.

Big Dreams

Around this time, two more extraordinary people came into my life. They weren't on the list Francis Chan wrote for me, but they've been influential for me just the same. One is a seventeen-year-old named Alex Sipala.

God certainly had a plan for the two of us to meet.

I had been invited to speak at the Activate Tour held over spring break in Myrtle Beach, South Carolina. Activate is a youth rally designed to call young people to action. Alex was backstage doing video interviews with all the speakers, so we began talking in the greenroom and hanging out. He had started this thing called the EU Movement (the name is taken from the Greek word *euodoo*, which can be translated "to have prosperous actions"), so I was asking him questions about it. It turned out that Alex and I were on the same page when it came to goals, thoughts, and dreams. Alex started the EU Movement to gather up young people who love God and want to live a life of action in response to that love.

A month later, I gave Alex a call to share with him an idea that had been growing inside of me. I shared a vision for what I was calling the Young and Beardless Community. It wasn't about a book or a marketing plan for me, but rather it was a website where young people could explore learning, growing, and doing. Soon Alex flew to Louisiana so we could shape and build the website together.

I love Alex's passion and energy. Our ultimate goals are similar: to make a difference by using what God has given us to advance His kingdom.

Remember at the beginning of the book when you asked

yourself, *What are you going to do with all this?* Well, Alex's response was this: "When we act on what God has done in us, and use that as a catalyst to spread change throughout our world, miracles happen."

He had already started the EU Movement to do just that, and that's why we have started the Young and Beardless Community as well—to inspire others to action. We want to give people resources like articles, interviews, and videos to equip them with all the tools they need to change the world.

God brought Alex into my life at the perfect time. We both believe that if you're big enough for your dream, then your dream isn't big enough for God. In other words, if your dream is big enough for you to handle alone and you don't need God, maybe you should dream bigger.

The Chalkboard

In our lives, we've got such an information overload going on that it's far too easy to miss something great—like life-changing people, places, or things.

While I was at the Activate Tour, I heard about a new church that had just opened called NewSpring. It was close to my hotel, so I decided to check it out. At that point, I'd never heard of the church or the founding pastor, Perry Noble.

Apparently, NewSpring in Myrtle Beach was one of the church's eleven campuses in South Carolina. This is what the church says about themselves on their website:

> Rather than being a building where people far from God are
> met with shame, guilt, and condemnation, Jesus leads us to

be a family that extends His grace, mercy, and forgiveness to everyone. No matter what you've been through or what questions you might have, we want you to be a part of the family.[2]

That sounded like the kind of church that I would want to check out, so I did. The sermon series they were in was called "I Love the '90s." Once again, sounded like something I would want to be a part of.

The service I attended was a week before Easter, so Pastor Noble asked everyone to invite people to go to church on Easter Sunday. (This was a satellite church, so we were watching him on the big screen.) He was creative with this request, though. He began talking about chalkboards. He'd grown up learning from teachers who wrote on them, so he walked over to a chalkboard he had on stage with him and wrote the following:

Passive ≠ Progress

Proactive = Progress

Simple, but effective! Pastor Noble went on to talk about the apostle Paul and how he spread the gospel. He then pointed out an important lesson from Paul's ministry: "Anytime we want to make progress in any area of our lives we're going to face opposition."[3]

He encouraged all of us in the church to stand up for what's right, even if it's politically incorrect and very unpopular. Pastor Noble stated that all of us have family members and friends and colleagues who aren't believers. Every day, we choose whether to be passive or proactive in sharing Jesus with them.

"Evangelism," Perry said, "is simply sharing the gospel with someone and then leaving it in God's hands." So he encouraged everybody to invite everyone they knew to come to the upcoming

Easter service. And the church gave us a tool to do this. Ushers passed out pieces of chalk. Perry encouraged us to write on sidewalks and buildings and give the whole state a chalk-invite to come to NewSpring on Easter.

After church, we went to a sushi place to have lunch. I spotted a Budweiser chalkboard in the corner with a 50 percent off ad written on it. When the hostess turned to seat us, I took my chalk and wrote, "Go to NewSpring for Easter" on the board. I hope no one was disappointed when they got to NewSpring and found out they weren't serving beer half off.

I took a picture of the board and tweeted it, and lo and behold, Perry Noble saw it and began a conversation with me. (Twitter. Ha!) Ultimately our Twitter conversation led to me meeting Perry, staying a weekend at his house, and touring NewSpring churches with him to see how God is working in South Carolina.

I'm so glad I stepped out to visit that church, literally walking through an open door to see what God might have planned. Since then, Pastor Noble has become a friend and mentor. He's one of the incredible believers God has brought into my path as I journey out into the world like Paul did, telling people about Jesus.

Who knew that chalk could be a game changer?

Around the Table

As you may know, meals are a big deal with the Robertson family. With so many wonderful cooks in our family and so many delicious recipes to choose from, I have a long list of memories surrounding the family dinner table. But one of the most meaningful is the rehearsal dinner for our wedding this past summer.

Mary Kate and I were getting married at our family's farm in the country. The events leading up to the big day were a lot like the year I'd just experienced: busy and moving and memorable. My whole family was together for a traditional rehearsal dinner, and different family members got up to give advice to us soon-to-be newlyweds.

Mamaw Kay started tearing up talking about me and sharing how happy she was for the two of us, since we were now committed for life. Seeing all the marriages represented around this table—my grandparents, parents, uncles, and aunts—confirmed that if people make Christ their priority, and put their faith and trust in Him, marriage can and will last through the tough times.

When my dad got up to make a toast, he tried to be tough, of course, but then the tears started rolling. We all know he's a big softie. He even joked about how he had made a vow not to cry at the wedding, so it looked like he was trying to get all the tears out that night. Then he blessed Mary Kate and me in the best way possible: by giving us encouragement and telling me how unique I was. Dad said that I am teaching him more than he's teaching me now. I was shocked—and very honored—to hear him say that, since he's been such an inspiration to me. I only pray that I can one day be the kind of dad to my children that my dad has been to my siblings and me.

All of our family meals, and the prayers we share before them, are modeled on what Jesus did His whole life. He didn't just walk around preaching to the masses. He didn't just go out and perform miracles, then slip back into some greenroom to hang out with the disciples. He lived and ate and breathed among the people He was speaking to. For centuries, real connections have been made around the dinner table. Mark 2 gives an example of this:

> Later, Levi invited Jesus and his disciples to his home as dinner guests, along with many tax collectors and other disreputable sinners. (There were many people of this kind among Jesus' followers.) But when the teachers of religious law who were Pharisees saw him eating with tax collectors and other sinners, they asked his disciples, "Why does he eat with such scum?" (vv. 15–16)

Jesus responded by saying that sick people need a doctor, not healthy people; and in the same way, He came to those who know they're sinners. (It turns out, that applies to all of us.)

We're all called to be a family. To come together and worship our Lord. He wants us to go out and sit among others who are different from us and start a relationship. To break bread. To have a conversation. I've seen this in person with people like Francis Chan and Perry Noble, and with friends like Alex Sipala.

I know that in this first year of college at Liberty University, life will change a lot. I'll meet many more new people as I travel along my path. I trust I will be able to walk alongside them and learn. I also hope to be able to walk alongside others and help them in whatever way they might need.

All of us are walking down a road in life, heading someplace. Even if you know where that place happens to be, you'll need to find friends to come with you. So stop to meet strangers when you see them. They might turn into your most trusted friends.

THINK ABOUT IT

1. What's your favorite "journey" story? Why is it your favorite?
2. Think about the hero of that story. Who were his or her companions? Why were they important?
3. Francis Chan gave me a list of people to meet and learn from. What did he say was so great about them? Are there people like that in your life you can get to know a little better?
4. Think back to when I said, "Who says you and I can't be one of those names someone scribbles on a piece of paper one day?" What do you think could make you "one of those names"?
5. How might sharing the gospel more actively change your journey and change the people you meet along the way?
6. How might being passive about sharing the gospel affect your journey and the people you meet?
7. People react to change in lots of different ways. How can change be an opportunity to walk alongside others and learn? Or to help them?

Book Highlight #11:

Oh, the Places You'll Go! by Dr. Seuss

Without Oh, the Places You'll Go!, *I wouldn't know I could move mountains.*

For all you less enthusiastic readers out there, here's the book for you. This Dr. Seuss book may appear childish, but its deep meaning puts it in the "adult-ish" category. It's got great nuggets like,

I'm afraid that *some* times
you'll play lonely games too.
Games you can't win
'cause you'll play against you.

Lines like this have challenged my thinking as much as some of the other books I've recommended. This book is written in true Dr. Seuss style, like *The Cat in the Hat* or *Green Eggs and Ham*, but its message is more serious. It's about the journey life takes us all on. It includes the ups and downs of life, like the line that says, "Kid, you'll move mountains," and the one above, which says that not all games can be won.

At my high school graduation party, my aunts performed a choral reading of it. I have to say, I was impressed. If you haven't read it yet, here's some advice from the book . . .

You're off to Great Places!
Today is your day!
Your mountain is waiting.
So . . . get on your way!"[4]

CHAPTER TWELVE

LOVING

(EVERYONE)

> God's definition of what matters is
> pretty straightforward. He measures
> our lives by how we love.
>
> —FRANCIS CHAN

SO JESUS LOVED . . .

There are some things in the Bible that we all like to debate about. For instance, the whole discussion around eschatology. *Eschatology* is a big word that means "the study of the end times"—the Rapture and the Second Coming and the Antichrist and what will happen pre-tribulation versus post-tribulation. It can be fun to talk about, but these mysterious subjects can also be a bit overwhelming when most of us have a tough time just living out the basics.

Some things in the Bible, however, are crystal clear. And one of these things is the subject of love.

What does love look like?

Jesus demonstrated what true love looks like, and He walked this earth touching, healing, and comforting those in need. He was the purest example of love *does*. He also gave precise commands on love, like this one:

> So now I am giving you a new commandment: Love each other. Just as I have loved you, you should love each other. Your love for one another will prove to the world that you are my disciples. (John 13:34–35)

Think about that verse. "Your love for one another will prove to the world that you are my disciples."

Gulp.

That means how I show love to others is how others will understand who God is.

That's challenging, isn't it? How do we put this verse in action? How do we show love? Not just *love* someone, but *show* them love. It's an action, isn't it?

Slow Down and Connect

Once when I was sixteen, I was out driving when I saw a kid my age walking along the side of the road without any shoes. He might have been just like me, inspired by a book to go running without shoes, but I had a feeling that wasn't the case. I slowed down and asked if he wanted a ride. At first he said no, but I eventually persuaded him to get in the Jeep.

This started a relationship. Over time I learned his story.

It turns out he had run away from home that day. Life with his family had been rough, to say the least: his parents were abusive and made poor decisions, which left his home hurt and broken. But his family had started to get help, even going to church to try and heal some of the brokenness. Even though his family was trying to recover from their trauma, this young man was still struggling.

Of course, I wanted him to come with us to church—to experience healing and peace. That seemed like a critical step. The church family I worship with is known for taking in the brokenhearted, and I knew he would find help there. But I didn't want to pressure him. Instead, I just tried to keep a casual connection with him and let God work through me.

A few years after we met, I discovered he was working at a grocery store. I tried to visit at least once a month to see how he was doing, just to talk and check in. But one day, I didn't see him working. Eventually I heard he had moved to Wisconsin, so I thought I might never see him again. Then, just recently, I bumped into him when I walked into a local restaurant and he was the host. He greeted me and told me he had gotten into witchcraft and that he had never actually moved to Wisconsin.

Just after I heard this, the youth minister at my home church, Nathan, walked into the same restaurant. So I told him the guy's story and asked if Nathan would try to begin a relationship with him. I knew I would be moving soon to go to college, and I worried that the guy would have no one checking on him. So Nathan reached out to him and began a friendship.

I have no idea where that guy is now, though I am on the lookout for him. But I do know that for once, the guy had someone who showed him love. Sometimes our encounters with others will be brief. But no matter the window of time you have together, you can show that person God's love, because God's love can live in the smallest of actions. We just need to slow down long enough to see who needs help. Like a ride. Or a meal. Or even a hug.

Written in Soap

There's a great line in the movie *My Best Friend's Wedding*.

Okay, I know it's a chick flick, but hear me out.

Julia Roberts's character, Julianne, is standing next to her best friend, Michael, on a boat ride just before Michael's big wedding. It just so happens that Julianne has fallen in love with Michael—but Michael doesn't know this, and he's marrying another woman. As the two stand on the boat, Michael leans over and says, "Kimmy [aka Michael's fiancée] says if you love someone you say it. You say it right then, out loud. Otherwise, the moment just—"

"Passes you by," Julianne replies.

"Passes you by. Yeah."[1]

And this is exactly what happens for Julianne.

She let many moments pass by without telling this man she loved him. And while love is an action, and technically actions are *supposed* to speak louder than words, sometimes you just have to spell it out for people. We're not all Einsteins (especially guys).

Words have meaning. Telling someone you love them is like covering them with a warm blanket on a cold day. It says someone cares about you.

Like most grandmas, 2-Mama has lots of stories about me

when I was a kid. The ones she loves the most seem to have to do with something sweet I did for her. (Hopefully she's forgotten all the times I wasn't sweet.) And she tells this particular story often.

Once 2-Mama was keeping all the grandkids for the weekend while all our parents were out of town. At seven years old I was the oldest, and there were five other kids there. That's six kids age seven or younger. Needless to say, 2-Mama had her hands full changing diapers, drying tears, and other stuff I don't even want to think about.

That night when she put me to sleep, she apologized that she hadn't spent any time with me that day. I told her it was okay and hugged her goodnight.

She says she went straight to bed exhausted from the busy day, but got up early the next morning to get a shower before the chaos started. When she opened the shower door, she got a big surprise. I had written "I love you, 2-Mama" over and over again in crayon soap on her shower walls. I'm sure I didn't realize it at the time, but I believe that when I saw how much my gesture meant to her, it compelled me from an early age to tell others I loved them too. That little act on my part made my grandma feel special.

I don't want to ever forget to tell someone I love them—it's such a small thing to express our feelings, especially when we see someone regularly, but it can make such an impact on the way people view themselves and the quality of relationships God has placed in their lives.

Invitations

Want to see the impact that other people have had in your life? Have a wedding.

When planning their wedding, one of the first tasks that a couple has to do is create the guest list. I took that job seriously, trying to include as many people who had shaped my life as possible, and my list kept growing. When we presented our lists to each other, Mary Kate had two hundred people on her list, and I had six hundred. She had told me she wanted a small wedding, and, like any guy, I just nodded and told her, "Okay."

Who knew "small" meant I couldn't have six hundred of my closest friends and family?

If you've never had to coordinate an event, the process of mailing invitations (like, actual snail mail) is actually pretty intense—especially since we can invite a thousand people to a Facebook event in two seconds flat. Not only do you have to come up with the text on the invitations (which you can't edit later, by the way—because paper), but you also have to *find out the mailing address* for each person. I don't know about you, but I don't carry around one of those little address books that used to be so common about thirty years ago. (Does anybody besides your grandma?)

But to be honest, I actually enjoyed working on the guest list. Because for each phone call I made to get a mailing address, for every invitation I stuffed in an envelope (and believe me—there were lots of stuffed envelopes), I recalled memories I had with each person and the role he or she had played in my life, whether big or small. And I realized something: God has blessed my life with so many wonderful people. At the beginning of the process, you wouldn't think that stuffing envelopes could be a humbling experience, but it really was.

I also realized how much more special our wedding day would be, because that day wasn't just about Mary Kate and me; it was about celebrating a love God had given us *and* celebrating the love so many others had shown us. Our love couldn't be possible without the love of others, who had shaped us into the people Mary Kate and I had become. And after I figured that out, I looked forward to seeing everyone at our wedding even more.

If there are three things I've always believed, they're these:

1. God is real, and He loves us.
2. If you stick with God, He will get you through those rough times you will eventually face.
3. Life is all about relationships. You need like-minded people to go on the journey with you.

Creating our guest list, which Mary Kate graciously agreed should include everyone, reminded me that I'm a part of a wonderful church full of family and friends. These people—these fellow travelers—bring so much strength to my life, and they make my life journey worthwhile.

Two Letters

Not too long ago, while putting a note in my toolbox, I spotted two old letters and pulled them out. One was from my mother. It was one of the encouraging notes she would occasionally write to remind me I was loved. She had written this particular letter before I'd left on a trip. As I read it again, I fought back tears:

John Luke:

Have I told you lately how proud I am of the man you've grown to become? I love how you honor God in all that you do, how you seek to know Him through His world, His Word, and His people. You are an awesome ambassador for Him. Thinking of this verse as I write this for you!

> I always thank my God as I remember you in my prayers, because I hear about your love for all his holy people and your faith in the Lord Jesus. I pray that your partnership with us in the faith may be effective in deepening your understanding of every good thing we share for the sake of Christ. Your love has given me great joy and encouragement, because you, brother, have refreshed the hearts of the Lord's people. (Philemon vv. 4–7 NIV)

So true! I love you, son. You are a fun, passionate, strong, kind, good, godly man. I will love you forever and always. Good times and bad, just like God loves you. You are my son, and for that I am thankful.

I will miss you this week!

Mom

Talk about a tear-jerker.

Around the time I was reading this letter, it had been a nerve-wracking couple of months. And just as I was preparing to enter a new stage in my life—getting married, moving away to college, and taking the first step toward adulthood—that letter reminded me how much my parents had shaped and molded me. I thank God for them daily, and I don't know what I would do without their encouragement.

The other letter I read had also been written before a trip. Mary Kate had given it to me before I went to Africa. It's a long letter, so I'm not going to include all of it here, but in it she basically told me to have fun and to make memories, and that she would miss me. She reminisced about the times we had already shared together, and then she wrote about how excited she was for our future.

The last bit of the letter really hit me in the heart:

> I love getting to know you more and more every day, and I know at the same time you are learning more about me. . . . Sometimes I think you know me better than I know myself. I saw a quote that said, "To be loved but not known is comforting but superficial. To be known and not loved is our greatest fear. But to be fully known and truly loved is, well, a lot like being loved by God."
>
> Just by loving you I feel like I have learned more about who God is—it's like experiencing Him in a whole new way . . . and I am amazed by it. Not only have I learned more about God, but more about myself and about what I am capable of.

Wow. Now you know one of the many reasons I fell in love with Mary Kate. What a deep thinker and a woman after God's own heart—and mine.

The quote Mary Kate shared was from a Timothy Keller book titled *The Meaning of Marriage*. I looked it up and read it in context:

> To be loved but not known is comforting but superficial. To be known and not loved is our greatest fear. But to be fully

known and truly loved is, well, a lot like being loved by God. It is what we need more than anything. It liberates us from pretense, humbles us out of our self-righteousness, and fortifies us for any difficulty life can throw at us.[2]

This kind of love is my greatest treasure. I'm thankful for the love my family shows me; it has made me who I am. Yet, as great as it is, human love isn't perfect.

Perfect love *does* exist, though. And it comes from our heavenly Father. As much as my mom and Mary Kate love me, God loves me even more. And He loves you too! It's the most intense love story ever told, the most meaningful redemption tale ever imagined. It's hard to describe such a big love, but God hints at it throughout the Bible:

- We are *known*, even down to the last hair on our heads (Luke 12:7).
- We are loved *unconditionally*, even more than a mother loves her child. God has even written our names on the palms of His hands (Isaiah 49:15–16).
- God considers us *wonderful*, and he takes pleasure in all the little details about us (Psalm 139:13–14).
- We are *treasured* so much that the greatest Man who ever lived thought we were worth dying for (John 3:16).

Yes, this love story is true, and it's bigger than we'll ever realize until we get to heaven. How awesome that we get to be on the receiving end of it!

The Greatest Story Ever Told

As the current president of Pixar (you lucky reader, we're going back to Pixar!) and Walt Disney Animation Studios, Ed Catmull is a guy who knows all about the power of storytelling—and, judging by the words from this 2015 speech, he treats stories as serious business: "It's going to be stories that change the world. How we communicate with people affects people. The real goal of what's [sic] Pixar is doing is to make the world a better place through storytelling."[3]

Catmull is right: stories *can* change the world. Every day, from TV news to our Facebook feeds, we're inundated with stories. Teachers often use stories to help us learn a lesson. (I mean, isn't that what the whole subject of *history* is, anyway?) Our families share anecdotes of memories and people of the past. We constantly relay to our friends things that have happened to us. And we can communicate our faith through stories too—God gave us a whole book of them to learn from.

The truth is, though, there's only one story that will change the world: a story of sacrificial love. No book, no movie, *nothing* can touch the majesty and earth-shattering power of that story.

And isn't it awesome that we're part of the greatest story ever told?

Add that to your spiritual IMDb page.

First Things First

On June 27, 2015, my best friend and I got married. And in typical Robertson fashion, my father surprised us before the ceremony . . . with a live mariachi band.

It's not as random as it sounds.

There's a Mexican restaurant down the street from my high school. During my high school years, the restaurant hosted a mariachi band. My friends and I loved to sing along with the band over our tacos and enchiladas. I can guarantee that you've never heard some of the top-forty hits covered the way that mariachi band did them! It was a great (and hilarious) surprise to see them as the pre-wedding entertainment on our special day.

Yes, I'll admit: Mary Kate and I are young to be getting married. But as I've mentioned, we have plenty of couples who have shown us how to love each other, that when you put God first in your marriage, good results are sure to follow. The secret to weathering our marriage together is something I believe C. S. Lewis once articulated in a letter he wrote:

> When I have learnt to love God better than my earthly dearest, I shall love my earthly dearest better than I do now. Insofar as I learn to love my earthly dearest at the expense of God and *instead* of God, I shall be moving towards the state in which I shall not love my earthly dearest at all. When first things are put first, second things are not suppressed but increased.[4]

First things first. And the first thing in both of our lives is God.

At the rehearsal dinner, Mary Kate's father shared that from the time she was born, he asked God to send Mary Kate a godly young man, someone who would love her and honor her and protect her and cherish her.

"And along comes John Luke," he said with a smile.

The only way those things can happen—the only way I can

do all of those things—is by loving and honoring our Lord. And by always remembering the definition of love: *selflessness*.

The opposite of love is selfishness.

We will have a learning curve, of course. Heading off to college, I'm sure we'll face new challenges and many times where we have to work hard on being selfless. But I do know this: I've married a woman who always puts God first, and I'm going to try my best to do the same. And if God is first in our lives, the rest will fall into place.

One Love

From a very early age, we learn that words are powerful. Words have the power to create new worlds (hello, books), stop wars, and revolutionize ways of thinking. Within just a few seconds, our own words can build someone up, but even more easily, our words can tear someone down.

For not having much mass, words wield a lot of power.

But have your words ever spoken something *into existence*?

Yeah. Didn't think so.

God's words are unfathomably powerful. Because when He says a word, all of a sudden things just *are* (Genesis 1:3).

But hey, we do our best to work with the English language.

I recently learned about a particularly special word while at a Passion, a youth conference held in various places in the US. The one I attended was in Atlanta, Georgia. I had the opportunity to hear Louie Giglio, pastor of the Passion City Church in Atlanta and the Passion conferences, share a message in which he stressed the importance of one word uttered by Jesus: *tetelestai*.

I had never heard this word, but it's a Greek word meaning

"it is finished." This is what Christ said on the cross just before He died.

Want to know the wonderful thing about what this means for us? When Jesus said, "It is finished," that actually meant the *beginning* for us. As Jesus breathed His last breath, we were able to breathe again as new creatures.

His death gave us new life.

His end made our beginnings possible.

And He did it with just one word.

We may not have the power to save the entire human race, but just as Jesus used His words to restore the lives of many, we can do the same with ours.

Dream House

I think this is what love looks like:

It's watching my Papaw Phil with Mamaw Kay. Knowing their story and having watched them my whole life, I can see that they're a testimony to God's goodness.

It's watching 2-Papa and 2-Mama, who are like second parents to me, two loving people who have always been there for me and my family. I can't imagine this life without them.

It was witnessing both sets of great-grandparents love each other until they left this earth for heaven.

It's seeing my mother love my dad and support each of her six children with equal importance.

It's having my father get teary-eyed at the wedding reception and telling me how glad he is for the guy I turned out to be.

It's seeing Uncle Al and Aunt Lisa fight for their marriage when it was in danger of being lost.

It's watching ministries like Camp Ch-Yo-Ca continue to grow because of the love for people my great-grandfather had.

It's witnessing, over and over again, the church family I have grown up in reach out and support missionaries all over the world, children who wouldn't have Christmas, the hungry, the poor, the drug addicted, the lost, and the brokenhearted.

Love is so many things.

Love is even hearing our wedding song sung by Ben Rector, my Frisbee-tossing friend I met in Canada.

Love is seeing Mary Kate in her wedding dress for the first time, knowing it was finally happening. Knowing it was real. I had thought I would marry her, I had talked about marrying her, and I had planned on marrying her. Then all the thoughts and plans and work had suddenly resulted in this day.

I'm finally marrying the love of my life. This is my dream.

It was also a reminder of God's love.

All of the events of the past year had led us to be together and were unmistakably divine. God is love. And God is faithful.

Since my dad officiated our wedding, he offered some suggestions on how to be successfully married. It turns out, it was not just good advice for marriage; it was good advice for any time of life. Yeah, I've told you a lot in this book about Mary Kate and our love story. But this is not a book about finding an awesome spouse (though I hope you do) or building a marriage (which you might not even be thinking about yet). It's about empowering you to follow your heart and your dreams, under the shadow of God's guidance and love.

As we prepared to say our vows and come together, Dad told us what he thought marriage (and life) looks like:

Marriage is a lot like building a house. It takes work. It can be stressful. So welcome to marriage. Unless you're Uncle Si, you probably don't talk to your house, and you'd never get angry with it. When something happens with your house, what do you do? You immediately try to get it fixed. Our house receives us every time we walk in, and keeps folks out that we don't want in, and it welcomes those in that we love. We care for it, we clean it, and we keep it nice. We're proud of our house. Build it on the Lord, and it will last.

To John Luke and Mary Kate, I'm so proud of you both, and I wish you all the best in life. May you be blessed with many children, wealth, and prosperity—but most importantly, the kind of happiness that can only come from the love of God and of each other.

I wish the same to all of you who've read about my journey. That house Dad was talking about—it doesn't just have to stand for a marriage. It could stand for your dream. Once you find that dream, grow into it, and start living it out, it's going to take some maintenance. But Dad's advice is to keep working at it. Care for it, keep it clean and nice, and bring people into it who will fill it with love. The love part—that's what makes a dream worth it. That's what keeps it going. If it's not built on God's love, your "dream house" won't make it. But if it is, it's a source of so much joy that it's worth all the work.

So here are my final words to you: good things happen to those who love each other and God, so be patient, because in the end it's all worth it.

Amen.

THINK ABOUT IT

1. God used a small act of love—like writing a little note on 2-Mama's shower—to start a chain reaction. Did someone ever show you a small act of love that led to something big later?

2. As you go about your day, try to think of at least three little ways to show some extra love to someone. Write them in your journal. Maybe months later you'll be able to look back and see how these acts of love have grown into something great!

3. Take a minute and write down as many people you love as you can think of. How can you show them love ASAP? A note? A quick hug? A letter or an act of service? Something silly, like writing with soap on a shower wall?

4. You might not be getting married anytime soon, but it's a fun exercise to think of who you'd want to have at your wedding and why. Make a fantasy list of everyone you'd want to invite (you too, guys), and reflect on how each person has shown you love.

5. For each person on your fantasy wedding guest list, take a moment to thank God for the love that person has shown you. How can you pass it on to someone else?

6. Why does love make for a good story? What about sacrificial love?

7. What part does love play in finding your dream? What does love add to your dream? Without it, what happens?

8. List some people who love well (do it and/or speak it) in your life. How do they show love?

Book Highlight #12

Crazy Love by Francis Chan

Without Crazy Love, *I never would have understood that convicts are just like you and me.*

Since you're at the end of this book, you already know I got to sit down with Francis Chan for breakfast. Twice. This guy is amazing for so many reasons, and I'm honored to have been able to sit with him. He is the former senior pastor of Cornerstone Church in Simi Valley, California. He lives life with an urgency partly because he's experienced great loss: first his mother, then his stepmother, and then his dad. All before he turned twelve.

In *Crazy Love*, Chan talks about the sorry state of lukewarm Christians and offers real-life stories of believers who have given it all for God. In his own crazy attempt at loving God, he tells about downsizing his home and giving away most of his possessions to the poor.

One of my favorite takeaways from the book is a section that talks about how the God of our universe—the creator of nitrogen, pine needles, galaxies, and E-minor—loves us with a radical, unconditional, self-sacrificing love. And how do we "honor" Him? We go to church, sing songs, and try not to cuss.

Wow.

We "sacrifice" so much, don't we? That section got me thinking, and hopefully it will get to you too.

WHAT GOD HAS PLANNED

Someone asked me a simple question recently. A question that hasn't been a loaded one until now:

"What have you been up to lately, John Luke?"

I smiled, knowing it was virtually impossible to sum it all up.

I could've told him about my travels and all the people I've met. I could've talked about falling in love, getting married, going on a honeymoon to Australia and Bora Bora. I could've talked about graduating from high school and heading off to my first year of college.

But instead, I just told him the truth.

"I've been seeing what God has planned for me."

So let's go back to where we started. What is your story? What kind of story do you want to tell ten years from now?

What action steps will you take to start living that story? What tools will you use, and who will you choose to walk alongside you? What fears will you overcome, and what places will you explore?

Most importantly, how will you share the greatest story of all, the story of Jesus Christ, with others along the way?

To review, let's look at everything we talked about in this book. I hope you've been able to put some of these tools in your own toolbox so you can start answering these questions:

- **Who Am I?** Knowing who you are is critical to where you're going. As you try to discover who you are, remember that, first and foremost, you are the child of the one true King. And that fact should affect your hopes and dreams. There are other ways you can discover who you are: embracing your physical family; connecting to a church family; analyzing your strengths and weaknesses, your likes and dislikes; and reading Scripture and applying it to your life. Discover your dreams though prayer and quiet reflection, and look for friends who will encourage you along the way. Work on your life story as if it's the next great novel. Chapter by chapter, put together a life that honors God, others, and yourself.

- **Where Am I Going?** Remember that even with the best of plans, God might intervene and call you to do something you never even dreamed possible. Keep your eyes, ears, and heart open. Stay curious—this means you have to actively look for ways God chooses to surprise you. Be rebellious against the things that are "normal" but not God-honoring. Take a stand when others won't—but if others do take a stand, join them. Support others who are doing the right thing.

- **What Am I Doing?** Failure is a part of life. It's completely unavoidable. But failure will not define you—getting back up will. When in doubt about your plans, look for your sand dollar moment, when God is nudging you toward something or someplace. And, above all else, love yourself and others with the same crazy love that God has for you.

Now, what are some other things *you* can do?

I'd like to invite you to join my community by visiting my website: youngandbeardless.com.

- I want to point you toward other resources that'll help you grow on your life journey. As I've said, I'm still learning, and my list of books will continue to grow. I've given you some good books to start with, but you'll find more resources on my website, plus podcasts, conferences, and more.
- I value your feedback. Please talk to me through my website or social media. I'm on Instagram @young_and_beardless and Twitter @John316Luke923.
- I want to encourage you to share what's in your toolbox with me and with others. We all learn differently; what has worked for you might be just the thing someone else needs to hear. Remember, you're exceptional, but not the exception. Someone else is going through what you're going through.

More on the Young and Beardless Community

When you get to my website, the first thing you read is this:

EMPOWERING YOU TO LIVE OUT YOUR DREAMS

Our mission is to help you make your dreams a reality by connecting you to others who believe as you do, are already doing what you dream of, or have a vision or resources for what you want to do. You're probably wondering who came up with this idea and why. You might be asking if anyone can start a movement. And those are good questions.

Allow me to answer them: my friends and I started this movement because we saw a need; and yes, anyone can do it.

Starting a movement is the easy part; continuing it is the challenge. Life has a way of interfering with the best intentions, so if you have a dream, know up front that it will require you to be deliberate and consistent and to work hard. Dreams are soft, fuzzy visions we have when we close our eyes, but turning dreams to reality requires our eyes to be open and our feet and hands to be ready to move. At Young and Beardless, we're ready to do the work required to help you be the best YOU possible.

ACKNOWLEDGMENTS

To all the folks at Thomas Nelson who saw my vision for this book and especially to Jennifer Gott, who has been there every step of the way.

To Travis, who helped put my words to paper.

To 2-Mama (Chrys Howard), who pushed me to keep writing and get it right.

To Mary Kate for loving me through it all and challenging me to be the best I can be.

To all the authors of all the books I've read that keep me growing and changing.

To my many friends and mentors, too many to name, but most of whom were written about in this book, who have been such an incredible part of my adventure so far.

To my great-grandparents and grandparents, who dreamed big first and paved the way for my dreams.

To my sisters, brothers, and cousins. I'm thankful I get to do life with you. It's never boring.

To my parents, whose constant encouragement and love for me has given me the freedom to grow.

ENDNOTES

Chapter 1: Knowing

1. Sean Covey, *The 7 Habits of Highly Effective Teens* (New York: Fireside, 1998), 20.
2. Erich Fromm, *To Have or to Be?* (London: Continuum, 1976, 2008), 89.
3. Rick Warren, "Believe You Are Who God Says You Are," *Daily Hope with Rick Warren*, 21 May 2014, http://rickwarren.org/devotional/english/believe-you-are-who-god-says-you-are (accessed January 15, 2016).
4. Francis Chan, *Crazy Love* (Colorado Springs: David C. Cook, 2013), 47.
5. Covey, *7 Habits*, 80.

Chapter 2: Dreaming

1. Steve Irwin, quoted on Australia Zoo, "Halogen National Young Leaders," http://www.australiazoo.com.au/education/events/. Originally from *Crikey! What an Adventure!* (TV movie), Dr. John Stainton, for Animal Planet.
2. You can still watch the ad on YouTube; just search "Think different ad" or visit

https://www.youtube.com/watch?gl=BE&v=dX9GTUMh490.

3. J. R. R. Tolkien, *The Hobbit* (New York: Ballantine, 1982), 4.

4. Tolkien, *The Fellowship of the Ring* (New York: Houghton Mifflin, 1954, 1994), 72.

5. Tolkien, *The Hobbit*, 19.

Chapter 3: Writing

1. Donald Miller, *A Million Miles in a Thousand Years: What I Learned While Editing My Life* (Nashville: Thomas Nelson, 2009), xiii.

2. Ibid., 179, emphasis added.

3. *It's a Wonderful Life*, directed by Frank Capra (Culver City: RKO Radio Pictures, 1946).

4. Andrew Stanton, "The Clues to a Great Story," *TED*, February 2012, https://www.ted.com/talks/andrew_stanton_the_clues_to_a_great_story?language=en.

5. Stanford Report, "'You've Got to Find What You Love,' Jobs Says," *Stanford News*, June 14, 2005, http://news.stanford.edu/news/2005/june15/jobs-061505.html.

6. John Steinbeck, *East of Eden* (New York: Penguin, 2002).

7. Miller, *A Million Miles*, 125.

8. Ibid., 108.

Chapter 4: Connecting

1. Chip Ingram, *Good to Great in God's Eyes: 10 Practices Great Christians Have in Common* (Grand Rapids, MI: Baker Books, 2007), 10.

2. Ibid., 12.

Chapter 5: Responding

1. Bob Goff, *Love Does* (Nashville: Thomas Nelson, 2012), xvi.

2. Ibid., 38.

3. Ibid., 69.

4. Ibid., 74.

5. There were that many in 2014, anyway. See "Number of Starbucks Stores Worldwide from 2003 to 2014," *Statista*, http://www.statista.com/statistics/266465/number-of-starbucks-stores-worldwide/ (accessed October 14, 2015).

6. "Company Information," Starbucks, http://www.starbucks.com/about-us/company-information (accessed October 14, 2015).

7. "What We Do," Restore International, http://restoreinternational.org/what-we-do/ (accessed October 14, 2015).

8. @BobGoff, Twitter, September 27, 2014, https://twitter.com/bobgoff/status/515911754581573632.

9. Goff, *Love Does*, 27.

10. Ibid., xiv.

11. Ibid., 144.

12. Ibid., 130.

13. Ibid., 155.

Chapter 7: Rebelling

1. Sarah Eekhoff Zylstra, "Alex and Brett Harris Are Doing Hard Things," *The Gospel Coalition*, November 5, 2014, http://www.thegospelcoalition.org/article/alex-and-brett-harris-are-doing-hard-things.

Chapter 8: Risking

1. Willie and Korie Robertson, with CNN's Kyra Phillips, "'Duck Dynasty' Star Stands by Beliefs," *CNN.com*, December 2013. http://www.cnn.com/2014/03/26/showbiz/tv/duck-dynasty-willie-robertson-new-day/index.html.

2. "'Duck Dynasty' Family: 'We Cannot Imagine the Show' Without Phil Robertson," *Hollywood Reporter*, December 19, 2013, http://www.hollywoodreporter.com/live-feed/duck-dynasty-family-we-cannot-667070.

3. Ibid.

4. Sean Hannity, quoted in Drew Menard, "TV and Radio Host

Sean Hannity Asks Students to Be Bold and Fix Our Nation," *Liberty University News & Events*, February 18, 2015, http://www.liberty.edu/news/index.cfm?PID=18495&MID=147201.

5. Ibid.

6. Rob Bell and Don Golden, *Jesus Wants to Save Christians* (Grand Rapids, MI: Zondervan, 2008), 167.

Chapter 9: Shining

1. Miller, *A Million Miles*, 125.

2. Ibid., 248.

3. Carla Hinton, "Ugandan Nun Included in *Time* Magazine's '100 Most Influential People' Issue Has Strong Oklahoma Ties," *Oklahoman*, April 24, 2014, http://newsok.com/article/4453618.

4. Goff, *Love Does*, xvi.

5. C. S. Lewis, *Mere Christianity* (San Francisco: HarperSanFrancisco, 1980), 97.

6. Dr. Seuss, *Oh, the Places You'll Go!* (New York: Random House Children's Books, 1960).

Chapter 10: Failing

1. Denver Scripps, "Theater Shooting Survivor Bonnie Kate Pourciau Zoghbi: God Sent Someone to Help Me," *Yahoo! News*, www.news.yahoo.com/video/theater-shooting-survivor-bonnie-kate-202439609.html.

2. Peter Baklinski, "Interview: 'I Do Forgive Him,' Says Teen with Knee Blown Apart by Aurora Theater Shooter," *LifeSite News*, August 13, 2012, https://www.lifesitenews.com/news/interview-i-do-forgive-him-says-teen-with-knee-blown-apart-by-aurora-theate.

3. Adventure Us, "Wildflower / A Proposal," YouTube, posted September 18, 2014, https://www.youtube.com/watch?v=kV5dMQ-432M.

4. Tolkien, *The Hobbit*, 69.

5. Mark Twain, *The Adventures of Huckleberry Finn* (Clayton, DE: Prestwick House, 2005), 144.
6. Ibid., 385.

Chapter 11: Going

1. "Overview," *ProjectBayview.com*, http://projectbayview.com (accessed October 14, 2015).
2. "About Us," *NewSpring Church*, https://newspring.cc/about (accessed October 14, 2015).
3. "I Love the '90s," *NewSpring Church*, https://newspring.cc/sermons/i-love-the-90s.
4. Dr. Suess, *Oh, the Places.*

Chapter 12: Loving

1. "Quotes for Michael O'Neal from *My Best Friend's Wedding*," IMDb, http://www.imdb.com/character/ch0010647/quotes.
2. Timothy Keller, *The Meaning of Marriage* (New York: Riverhead Books, 2013), 89.
3. Ed Catmull, speaking at the Willow Creek Global Leadership Summit, South Barrington, IL, August 6, 2015. http://chuckscoggins.com/blog/2015/08/06/the-global-leadership-summit-session-two-ed-catmull/.
4. C. S. Lewis, *Letters of C. S. Lewis*, rev. and exp., ed. Walter Hooper (New York: HarperCollins, 1966), 429.